Record of Buddhistic Kingdoms

by Fa Hien

Translated by James Legge

PREFACE

Several times during my long residence in Hong Kong I endeavoured to read through the "Narrative of Fa-hien;" but though interested with the graphic details of much of the work, its columns bristled so constantly--now with his phonetic representations of Sanskrit words, and now with his substitution for them of their meanings in Chinese characters, and I was, moreover, so much occupied with my own special labours on the Confucian Classics, that my success was far from satisfactory. When Dr. Eitel's "Handbook for the Student of Chinese Buddhism" appeared in 1870, the difficulty occasioned by the Sanskrit words and names was removed, but the other difficulty remained; and I was not able to look into the book again for several years. Nor had I much inducement to do so in the two copies of it which I had been able to procure, on poor paper, and printed from blocks badly cut at first, and so worn with use as to yield books the reverse of attractive in their appearance to the student.

In the meantime I kept studying the subject of Buddhism from various sources; and in 1878 began to lecture, here in Oxford, on the Travels with my Davis Chinese scholar, who was at the same time Boden Sanskrit scholar. As we went on, I wrote out a translation in English for my own satisfaction of nearly half the narrative. In the beginning of last year I made Fa-hien again the subject of lecture, wrote out a second translation, independent of the former, and pushed on till I had completed the whole.

The want of a good and clear text had been supplied by my friend, Mr. Bunyiu Nanjio, who sent to me from Japan a copy, the text of which is appended to the translation and notes, and of the nature of which some account is given in the Introduction, and towards the end of this Preface.

The present work consists of three parts: the Translation of Fa-hien's Narrative of his Travels; copious Notes; and the Chinese Text of my copy from Japan.

It is for the Translation that I hold myself more especially responsible. Portions of it were written out three times, and the whole of it twice. While preparing my own version I made frequent reference to previous translations:--those of M. Abel Remusat, "Revu, complete, et augmente d'eclaircissements nouveaux par MM. Klaproth et Landress" (Paris, 1836); of the Rev. Samuel Beal (London, 1869), and his revision of it, prefixed to his "Buddhist Records of the Western World" (Trubner's Oriental Series, 1884); and of Mr. Herbert A. Giles, of H.M.'s Consular Service in China (1877). To these I have to add a series of articles on "Fa-hsien and his English Translators," by Mr. T. Watters, British Consul at I-Chang (China Review, 1879, 1880). Those articles are of the highest value, displaying accuracy of Chinese scholarship and an extensive knowledge of Buddhism. I have regretted that Mr. Watters, while reviewing others, did not himself write out and publish a version of the whole of Fa-hien's narrative. If he had done so, I should probably have thought that, on the whole, nothing more remained to be done for the distinguished Chinese pilgrim in the way of translation. Mr. Watters had to judge of the comparative merits of the versions of Beal and Giles, and pronounce on the many points of contention between them. I have endeavoured to eschew those matters, and have seldom made remarks of a critical nature in defence of renderings of my own.

The Chinese narrative runs on without any break. It was Klaproth who divided Remusat's translation into forty chapters. The division is helpful to the reader, and I have followed it excepting in three or four instances. In the reprinted Chinese text the chapters are separated by a circle in the column.

In transliterating the names of Chinese characters I have generally followed the spelling of Morrison rather than the Pekinese, which is now in vogue. We cannot tell exactly what the pronunciation of them was, about fifteen hundred years ago, in the time of Fa-hien; but the southern mandarin must be a shade nearer to it than that of Peking at the present day. In transliterating the Indian names I have for the most part followed Dr. Eitel, with such modification as seemed good and in harmony with growing usage.

For the Notes I can do little more than claim the merit of selection and condensation. My first object in them was to explain what in the text required explanation to an English reader. All Chinese texts, and Buddhist

3

texts especially, are new to foreign students. One has to do for them what many hundreds of the ablest scholars in Europe have done for the Greek and Latin Classics during several hundred years, and what the thousands of critics and commentators have been doing of our Sacred Scriptures for nearly eighteen centuries. There are few predecessors in the field of Chinese literature into whose labours translators of the present century can enter. This will be received, I hope, as a sufficient apology for the minuteness and length of some of the notes. A second object in them was to teach myself first, and then others, something of the history and doctrines of Buddhism. I have thought that they might be learned better in connexion with a lively narrative like that of Fa-hien than by reading didactic descriptions and argumentative books. Such has been my own experience. The books which I have consulted for these notes have been many, besides Chinese works. My principal help has been the full and masterly handbook of Eitel, mentioned already, and often referred to as E.H. Spence Hardy's "Eastern Monachism" (E.M.) and "Manual of Buddhism" (M.B.) have been constantly in hand, as well as Rhys Davids' Buddhism, published by the Society for Promoting Christian Knowledge, his Hibbert Lectures, and his Buddhist Suttas in the Sacred Books of the East, and other writings. I need not mention other authorities, having endeavoured always to specify them where I make use of them. My proximity and access to the Bodleian Library and the Indian Institute have been of great advantage.

I may be allowed to say that, so far as my own study of it has gone, I think there are many things in the vast field of Buddhist literature which still require to be carefully handled. How far, for instance, are we entitled to regard the present Sutras as genuine and sufficiently accurate copies of those which were accepted by the Councils before our Christian era? Can anything be done to trace the rise of the legends and marvels of Sakyamuni's history, which were current so early (as it seems to us) as the time of Fa-hien, and which startle us so frequently by similarities between them and narratives in our Gospels? Dr. Hermann Oldenberg, certainly a great authority on Buddhistic subjects, says that "a biography of Buddha has not come down to us from ancient times, from the age of the Pali texts; and, we can safely say, no such biography existed then" ("Buddha--His Life, His Doctrine, His Order," as translated by Hoey, p. 78). He has also (in the same work, pp. 99,

416, 417) come to the conclusion that the hitherto unchallenged tradition that the Buddha was "a king's son" must be given up. The name "king's son" (in Chinese {...}), always used of the Buddha, certainly requires to be understood in the highest sense. I am content myself to wait for further information on these and other points, as the result of prolonged and careful research.

Dr. Rhys Davids has kindly read the proofs of the Translation and Notes, and I most certainly thank him for doing so, for his many valuable corrections in the Notes, and for other suggestions which I have received from him. I may not always think on various points exactly as he does, but I am not more forward than he is to say with Horace,--

"Nullius addictus jurare in verba magistri."

I have referred above, and also in the Introduction, to the Corean text of Fa-hien's narrative, which I received from Mr. Nanjio. It is on the whole so much superior to the better-known texts, that I determined to attempt to reproduce it at the end of the little volume, so far as our resources here in Oxford would permit. To do so has not been an easy task. The two fonts of Chinese types in the Clarendon Press were prepared primarily for printing the translation of our Sacred Scriptures, and then extended so as to be available for printing also the Confucian Classics; but the Buddhist work necessarily requires many types not found in them, while many other characters in the Corean recension are peculiar in their forms, and some are what Chinese dictionaries denominate "vulgar." That we have succeeded so well as we have done is owing chiefly to the intelligence, ingenuity, and untiring attention of Mr. J. C. Pembrey, the Oriental Reader.

The pictures that have been introduced were taken from a superb edition of a History of Buddha, republished recently at Hang-chau in Cheh-kiang, and profusely illustrated in the best style of Chinese art. I am indebted for the use of it to the Rev. J. H. Sedgwick, University Chinese Scholar.

James Legge.

Oxford: June, 1886.

The accompanying Sketch-Map, taken in connexion with the notes on the different places in the Narrative, will give the reader a sufficiently accurate knowledge of Fa-hien's route.

There is no difficulty in laying it down after he crossed the Indus from east to west into the Punjab, all the principal places, at which he touched or rested, having been determined by Cunningham and other Indian geographers and archaeologists. Most of the places from Ch'ang- an to Bannu have also been identified. Woo-e has been put down as near Kutcha, or Kuldja, in 43d 25s N., 81d 15s E. The country of K'ieh-ch'a was probably Ladak, but I am inclined to think that the place where the traveller crossed the Indus and entered it must have been further east than Skardo. A doubt is intimated on page 24 as to the identification of T'o-leih with Darada, but Greenough's "Physical and Geological Sketch-Map of British India" shows "Dardu Proper," all lying on the east of the Indus, exactly in the position where the Narrative would lead us to place it. The point at which Fa-hien recrossed the Indus into Udyana on the west of it is unknown. Takshasila, which he visited, was no doubt on the west of the river, and has been incorrectly accepted as the Taxila of Arrian in the Punjab. It should be written Takshasira, of which the Chinese phonetisation will allow;--see a note of Beal in his "Buddhist Records of the Western World," i. 138.

We must suppose that Fa-hien went on from Nan-king to Ch'ang-an, but the Narrative does not record the fact of his doing so.

INTRODUCTION

Life of Fa-Hien; Genuineness and Integrity of the Text of his Narrative; Number of the Adherents of Buddhism.

1. Nothing of great importance is known about Fa-hien in addition to what may be gathered from his own record of his travels. I have read the accounts of him in the "Memoirs of Eminent Monks," compiled in A.D. 519, and a later work, the "Memoirs of Marvellous Monks," by the third emperor of the Ming dynasty (A.D. 1403-1424), which, however, is nearly all borrowed from the other; and all in them that has an appearance of verisimilitude can be brought within brief compass.

His surname, they tell us, was Kung, and he was a native of Wu-yang in P'ing-Yang, which is still the name of a large department in Shan-hsi. He had three brothers older than himself; but when they all died before shedding their first teeth, his father devoted him to the service of the Buddhist society, and had him entered as a Sramanera, still keeping him at home in the family. The little fellow fell dangerously ill, and the father sent him to the monastery, where he soon got well and refused to return to his parents.

When he was ten years old, his father died; and an uncle, considering the widowed solitariness and helplessness of the mother, urged him to renounce the monastic life, and return to her, but the boy replied, "I did not quit the family in compliance with my father's wishes, but because I wished to be far from the dust and vulgar ways of life. This is why I chose monkhood." The uncle approved of his words and gave over urging him. When his mother also died, it appeared how great had been the affection for her of his fine nature; but after her burial he returned to the monastery.

On one occasion he was cutting rice with a score or two of his fellow-disciples, when some hungry thieves came upon them to take away their grain by force. The other Sramaneras all fled, but our young hero stood his ground, and said to the thieves, "If you must have the grain, take what you please. But, Sirs, it was your former neglect of charity which brought you to your present state of destitution; and now, again, you wish to rob others. I am afraid that in the coming ages you will have still greater poverty and distress;--I am sorry for you beforehand." With these words he followed his companions into the monastery, while the thieves left the grain and went away, all the monks, of whom there were several hundred, doing homage to his conduct and courage.

When he had finished his noviciate and taken on him the obligations of the full Buddhist orders, his earnest courage, clear intelligence, and strict regulation of his demeanour were conspicuous; and soon after, he undertook his journey to India in search of complete copies of the Vinaya-pitaka. What follows this is merely an account of his travels in India and return to China by sea, condensed from his own narrative, with the addition of some marvellous incidents that happened to him, on his visit to the Vulture Peak near Rajagriha.

It is said in the end that after his return to China, he went to the capital (evidently Nanking), and there, along with the Indian Sramana Buddha-bhadra, executed translations of some of the works which he had obtained in India; and that before he had done all that he wished to do in this way, he removed to King-chow (in the present Hoo-pih), and died in the monastery of Sin, at the age of eighty-eight, to the great sorrow of all who knew him. It is added that there is another larger work giving an account of his travels in various countries.

Such is all the information given about our author, beyond what he himself has told us. Fa-hien was his clerical name, and means "Illustrious in the Law," or "Illustrious master of the Law." The Shih which often precedes it is an abbreviation of the name of Buddha as Sakyamuni, "the Sakya, mighty in Love, dwelling in Seclusion and Silence," and may be taken as equivalent to Buddhist. It is sometimes said to have belonged to "the eastern Tsin dynasty" (A.D. 317-419), and sometimes to "the Sung," that is, the Sung dynasty of the House of Liu (A.D. 420-478). If he became a full monk at the age of twenty, and went to India when he was twenty-five, his long life may have been divided pretty equally between the two dynasties.

2. If there were ever another and larger account of Fa-hien's travels than the

narrative of which a translation is now given, it has long ceased to be in existence.

In the Catalogue of the imperial library of the Suy dynasty (A.D. 589- 618), the name Fa-hien occurs four times. Towards the end of the last section of it (page 22), after a reference to his travels, his labours in translation at Kin-ling (another name for Nanking), in conjunction with Buddha-bhadra, are described. In the second section, page 15, we find "A Record of Buddhistic Kingdoms;"--with a note, saying that it was the work of the "Sramana, Fa-hien;" and again, on page 13, we have "Narrative of Fa-hien in two Books," and "Narrative of Fa-hien's Travels in one Book." But all these three entries may possibly belong to different copies of the same work, the first and the other two being in separate subdivisions of the Catalogue.

In the two Chinese copies of the narrative in my possession the title is "Record of Buddhistic Kingdoms." In the Japanese or Corean recension subjoined to this translation, the title is twofold; first, "Narrative of the Distinguished Monk, Fa-hien;" and then, more at large, "Incidents of Travels in India, by the Sramana of the Eastern Tsin, Fa-hien, recorded by himself."

There is still earlier attestation of the existence of our little work than the Suy Catalogue. The Catalogue Raisonne of the imperial library of the present dynasty (chap. 71) mentions two quotations from it by Le Tao-yuen, a geographical writer of the dynasty of the Northern Wei (A.D. 386-584), one of them containing 89 characters, and the other 276; both of them given as from the "Narrative of Fa-hien."

In all catalogues subsequent to that of Suy our work appears. The evidence for its authenticity and genuineness is all that could be required. It is clear to myself that the "Record of Buddhistic Kingdoms" and the "Narrative of his Travels by Fa-hien" were designations of one and the same work, and that it is doubtful whether any larger work on the same subject was ever current. With regard to the text subjoined to my translation, it was published in Japan in 1779. The editor had before him four recensions of the narrative; those of the Sung and Ming dynasties, with appendixes on the names of certain characters in them; that of Japan; and that of Corea. He wisely adopted the

Corean text, published in accordance with a royal rescript in 1726, so far as I can make out; but the different readings of the other texts are all given in top-notes, instead of foot-notes as with us, this being one of the points in which customs in the east and west go by contraries. Very occasionally, the editor indicates by a single character, equivalent to "right" or "wrong," which reading in his opinion is to be preferred. In the notes to the present republication of the Corean text, S stands for Sung, M for Ming, and J for Japanese; R for right, and W for wrong. I have taken the trouble to give all the various readings (amounting to more than 300), partly as a curiosity and to make my text complete, and partly to show how, in the transcription of writings in whatever language, such variations are sure to occur,

"maculae, quas aut incuria fudit, Aut humana parum cavit nature,"

while on the whole they very slightly affect the meaning of the document.

The editors of the Catalogue Raisonne intimate their doubts of the good taste and reliability of all Fa-hien's statements. It offends them that he should call central India the "Middle Kingdom," and China, which to them was the true and only Middle Kingdom, but "a Border land;"--it offends them as the vaunting language of a Buddhist writer, whereas the reader will see in the expressions only an instance of what Fa-hien calls his "simple straightforwardness."

As an instance of his unreliability they refer to his account of the Buddhism of Khoten, whereas it is well known, they say, that the Khoteners from ancient times till now have been Mohammedans;--as if they could have been so 170 years before Mohammed was born, and 222 years before the year of the Hegira! And this is criticism in China. The Catalogue was ordered by the K'ien-lung emperor in 1722. Between three and four hundred of the "Great Scholars" of the empire were engaged on it in various departments, and thus egregiously ignorant did they show themselves of all beyond the limits of their own country, and even of the literature of that country itself.

Much of what Fa-hien tells his readers of Buddhist miracles and legends is indeed unreliable and grotesque; but we have from him the truth as to what

10

he saw and heard.

3. In concluding this introduction I wish to call attention to some estimates of the number of Buddhists in the world which have become current, believing, as I do, that the smallest of them is much above what is correct.

i. In a note on the first page of his work on the Bhilsa Topes (1854), General Cunningham says: "The Christians number about 270 millions; the Buddhists about 222 millions, who are distributed as follows:-- China 170 millions, Japan 25, Anam 14, Siam 3, Ava 8, Nepal 1, and Ceylon 1; total, 222 millions."

ii. In his article on M. J. Barthelemy Saint Hilaire's "Le Bouddha et sa Religion," republished in his "Chips from a German Workshop," vol. i. (1868), Professor Max Muller (p. 215) says, "The young prince became the founder of a religion which, after more than two thousand years, is still professed by 455 millions of human beings," and he appends the following note: "Though truth is not settled by majorities, it would be interesting to know which religion counts at the present moment the largest numbers of believers. Berghaus, in his 'Physical Atlas,' gives the following division of the human race according to religion:--'Buddhists 31.2 per cent, Christians 30.7, Mohammedans 15.7, Brahmanists 13.4, Heathens 8.7, and Jews 0.3.' As Berghaus does not distinguish the Buddhists in China from the followers of Confucius and Laotse, the first place on the scale really belongs to Christianity. It is difficult to say to what religion a man belongs, as the same person may profess two or three. The emperor himself, after sacrificing according to the ritual of Confucius, visits a Tao-sse temple, and afterwards bows before an image of Fo in a Buddhist chapel. ('Melanges Asiatiques de St. Petersbourg,' vol. ii. p. 374.)"

iii. Both these estimates are exceeded by Dr. T. W. Rhys Davids (intimating also the uncertainty of the statements, and that numbers are no evidence of truth) in the introduction to his "Manual of Buddhism." The Buddhists there appear as amounting in all to 500 millions:--30 millions of Southern Buddhists, in Ceylon, Burma, Siam, Anam, and India (Jains); and 470 millions of North Buddhists, of whom nearly 33 millions are assigned to

11

Japan, and 414,686,974 to the eighteen provinces of China proper. According to him, Christians amount to about 26 per cent of mankind, Hindus to about 13, Mohammedans to about 12 1/2, Buddhists to about 40, and Jews to about 1/2.

In regard to all these estimates, it will be observed that the immense numbers assigned to Buddhism are made out by the multitude of Chinese with which it is credited. Subtract Cunningham's 170 millions of Chinese from his total of 222, and there remains only 52 millions of Buddhists. Subtract Davids' (say) 414 1/2 millions of Chinese from his total of 500, and there remain only 85 1/2 millions for Buddhism. Of the numbers assigned to other countries, as well as of their whole populations, I am in considerable doubt, excepting in the cases of Ceylon and India; but the greatness of the estimates turns upon the immense multitudes said to be in China. I do not know what total population Cunningham allowed for that country, nor on what principal he allotted 170 millions of it to Buddhism;--perhaps he halved his estimate of the whole, whereas Berghaus and Davids allotted to it the highest estimates that have been given of the people.

But we have no certain information of the population of China. At an interview with the former Chinese ambassador, Kwo Sung-tao, in Paris, in 1878, I begged him to write out for me the amount, with the authority for it, and he assured me that it could not be done. I have read probably almost everything that has been published on the subject, and endeavoured by methods of my own to arrive at a satisfactory conclusion;--without reaching a result which I can venture to lay before the public. My impression has been that 400 millions is hardly an exaggeration.

But supposing that we had reliable returns of the whole population, how shall we proceed to apportion that among Confucianists, Taoists, and Buddhists? Confucianism is the orthodoxy of China. The common name for it is Ju Chiao, "the Doctrines held by the Learned Class," entrance into the circle of which is, with a few insignificant exceptions, open to all the people. The mass of them and the masses under their influence are preponderatingly Confucian; and in the observance of ancestral worship, the most remarkable feature of the religion proper of China from the earliest times, of which

12

Confucius was not the author but the prophet, an overwhelming majority are regular and assiduous.

Among "the strange principles" which the emperor of the K'ang-hsi period, in one of his famous Sixteen Precepts, exhorted his people to "discountenance and put away, in order to exalt the correct doctrine," Buddhism and Taoism were both included. If, as stated in the note quoted from Professor Muller, the emperor countenances both the Taoist worship and the Buddhist, he does so for reasons of state;--to please especially his Buddhist subjects in Thibet and Mongolia, and not to offend the many whose superstitious fancies incline to Taoism.

When I went out and in as a missionary among the Chinese people for about thirty years, it sometimes occurred to me that only the inmates of their monasteries and the recluses of both systems should be enumerated as Buddhists and Taoists; but I was in the end constrained to widen that judgment, and to admit a considerable following of both among the people, who have neither received the tonsure nor assumed the yellow top. Dr. Eitel, in concluding his discussion of this point in his "Lecture on Buddhism, an Event in History," says: "It is not too much to say that most Chinese are theoretically Confucianists, but emotionally Buddhists or Taoists. But fairness requires us to add that, though the mass of the people are more or less influenced by Buddhist doctrines, yet the people, as a whole, have no respect for the Buddhist church, and habitually sneer at Buddhist priests." For the "most" in the former of these two sentences I would substitute "nearly all;" and between my friend's "but" and "emotionally" I would introduce "many are," and would not care to contest his conclusion farther. It does seem to me preposterous to credit Buddhism with the whole of the vast population of China, the great majority of whom are Confucianists. My own opinion is, that its adherents are not so many as those even of Mohammedanism, and that instead of being the most numerous of the religions (so called) of the world, it is only entitled to occupy the fifth place, ranking below Christianity, Confucianism, Brahmanism, and Mohammedanism, and followed, some distance off, by Taoism. To make a table of per-centages of mankind, and assign to each system its proportion, is to seem to be wise where we are deplorably ignorant; and, moreover, if our

13

means of information were much better than they are, our figures would merely show the outward adherence. A fractional per-centage might tell more for one system than a very large integral one for another.

THE

TRAVELS OF FA-HIEN

or

RECORD OF BUDDHISTIC KINGDOMS

CHAPTER I

FROM CH'ANG-GAN TO THE SANDY DESERT

Fa-hien had been living in Ch'ang-gan.[1] Deploring the mutilated and imperfect state of the collection of the Books of Discipline, in the second year of the period Hwang-che, being the Ke-hae year of the cycle,[2] he entered into an engagement with Kwuy-king, Tao-ching, Hwuy-ying, and Hwuy-wei,[3] that they should go to India and seek for the Disciplinary Rules.[4]

After starting from Ch'ang-gan, they passed through Lung,[5] and came to the kingdom of K'een-kwei,[6] where they stopped for the summer retreat.[7] When that was over, they went forward to the kingdom of Now-t'an,[8] crossed the mountain of Yang-low, and reached the emporium of Chang-yih.[9] There they found the country so much disturbed that travelling on the roads was impossible for them. Its king, however, was very attentive to them, kept them (in his capital), and acted the part of their danapati.[10]

Here they met with Che-yen, Hwuy-keen, Sang-shao, Pao-yun, and Sang-king;[11] and in pleasant association with them, as bound on the same journey with themselves, they passed the summer retreat (of that year)[12] together, resuming after it their travelling, and going on to T'un-hwang,[13] (the chief town) in the frontier territory of defence extending for about 80 le from east to west, and about 40 from north to south. Their company, increased as it had been, halted there for some days more than a month, after which Fa-hien and his four friends started first in the suite of an envoy,[14] having separated (for a time) from Pao-yun and his associates.

Le Hao,[15] the prefect of T'un-hwang, had supplied them with the means of crossing the desert (before them), in which there are many evil demons and hot winds. (Travellers) who encounter them perish all to a man. There is not a bird to be seen in the air above, nor an animal on the ground below. Though you look all round most earnestly to find where you can cross, you know not where to make your choice, the only mark and indication being the dry bones of the dead (left upon the sand).[16]

NOTES

[1] Ch'ang-gan is still the name of the principal district (and its city) in the department of Se-gan, Shen-se. It had been the capital of the first empire of Han (B.C. 202-A.D. 24), as it subsequently was that of Suy (A.D. 589-618). The empire of the eastern Tsin, towards the close of which Fa-hien lived, had its capital at or near Nan-king, and Ch'ang-gan was the capital of the principal of the three Ts'in kingdoms, which, with many other minor ones, maintained a semi- independence of Tsin, their rulers sometimes even assuming the title of emperor.

[2] The period Hwang-che embraced from A.D. 399 to 414, being the greater portion of the reign of Yao Hing of the After Ts'in, a powerful prince. He adopted Hwang-che for the style of his reign in 399, and the cyclical name of that year was Kang-tsze. It is not possible at this distance of time to explain, if it could be explained, how Fa-hien came to say that Ke-hae was the second year of the period. It seems most reasonable to suppose that he set out on his pilgrimage in A.D. 399, the cycle name of which was Ke-hae, as {.}, the second year, instead of {.}, the first, might easily creep into the text. In the "Memoirs of Eminent Monks" it is said that our author started in the third year of the period Lung-gan of the eastern Tsin, which was A.D. 399.

[3] These, like Fa-hien itself, are all what we might call "clerical" names, appellations given to the parties as monks or sramanas.

16

[4] The Buddhist tripitaka or canon consists of three collections, containing, according to Eitel (p. 150), "doctrinal aphorisms (or statements, purporting to be from Buddha himself); works on discipline; and works on metaphysics:"--called sutra, vinaya, and abhidharma; in Chinese, king {.}, leuh {.}, and lun {.}, or texts, laws or rules, and discussions. Dr. Rhys Davids objects to the designation of "metaphysics" as used of the abhidharma works, saying that "they bear much more the relation to 'dharma' which 'by-law' bears to 'law' than that which 'metaphysics' bears to 'physics'" (Hibbert Lectures, p. 49). However this be, it was about the vinaya works that Fa-hien was chiefly concerned. He wanted a good code of the rules for the government of "the Order" in all its internal and external relations.

[5] Lung embraced the western part of Shen-se and the eastern part of Kan-suh. The name remains in Lung Chow, in the extreme west of Shen-se.

[6] K'een-kwei was the second king of "the Western Ts'in." His family was of northern or barbarous origin, from the tribe of the Seen-pe, with the surname of K'eih-fuh. The first king was Kwo-kin, and received his appointment from the sovereign of the chief Ts'in kingdom in 385. He was succeeded in 388 by his brother, the K'een-kwei of the text, who was very prosperous in 398, and took the title of king of Ts'in. Fa-hien would find him at his capital, somewhere in the present department of Lan-chow, Kan-suh.

[7] Under varshas or vashavasana (Pali, vassa; Spence Hardy, vass), Eitel (p. 163) says:--"One of the most ancient institutions of Buddhist discipline, requiring all ecclesiastics to spend the rainy season in a monastery in devotional exercises. Chinese Buddhists naturally substituted the hot season for the rainy (from the 16th day of the 5th to the 15th of the 9th Chinese month)."

[8] During the troubled period of the Tsin dynasty, there were five (usurping) Leang sovereignties in the western part of the empire ({.} {.}). The name Leang remains in the department of Leang-chow in the northern part of Kan-suh. The "southern Leang" arose in 397 under a Tuh-fah Wu-ku, who was succeeded in 399 by a brother, Le-luh-koo; and he again by his brother, the Now-t'an of the text, in 402, who was not yet king therefore

when Fa-hien and his friends reached his capital. How he is represented as being so may be accounted for in various ways, of which it is not necessary to write.

[9] Chang-yih is still the name of a district in Kan-chow department, Kan-suh. It is a long way north and west from Lan-chow, and not far from the Great Wall. Its king at this time was, probably, Twan-yeh of "the northern Leang."

[10] Dana is the name for religious charity, the first of the six paramitas, or means of attaining to nirvana; and a danapati is "one who practises dana and thereby crosses {.} the sea of misery." It is given as "a title of honour to all who support the cause of Buddhism by acts of charity, especially to founders and patrons of monasteries;"--see Eitel, p. 29.

[11] Of these pilgrims with their clerical names, the most distinguished was Pao-yun, who translated various Sanskrit works on his return from India, of which only one seems to be now existing. He died in 449. See Nanjio's Catalogue of the Tripitaka, col. 417.

[12] This was the second summer since the pilgrims left Ch'ang-gan. We are now therefore, probably, in A.D. 400.

[13] T'un-hwang (lat. 39d 40s N.; lon. 94d 50s E.) is still the name of one of the two districts constituting the department of Gan-se, the most western of the prefectures of Kan-suh; beyond the termination of the Great Wall.

[14] Who this envoy was, and where he was going, we do not know. The text will not admit of any other translation.

[15] Le Hao was a native of Lung-se, a man of learning, able and kindly in his government. He was appointed governor or prefect of T'un-hwang by the king of "the northern Leang," in 400; and there he sustained himself, becoming by and by "duke of western Leang," till he died in 417.

[16] "The river of sand;" the great desert of Kobi or Gobi; having various

other names. It was a great task which the pilgrims had now before them,--to cross this desert. The name of "river" in the Chinese misleads the reader, and he thinks of crossing it as of crossing a stream; but they had to traverse it from east to west. In his "Vocabulary of Proper Names," p. 23, Dr. Porter Smith says:--"It extends from the eastern frontier of Mongolia, south-westward to the further frontier of Turkestan, to within six miles of Ilchi, the chief town of Khoten. It thus comprises some twenty-three degrees of longitude in length, and from three to ten degrees of latitude in breadth, being about 2,100 miles in its greatest length. In some places it is arable. Some idea may be formed of the terror with which this 'Sea of Sand,' with its vast billows of shifting sands, is regarded, from the legend that in one of the storms 360 cities were all buried within the space of twenty-four hours." So also Gilmour's "Among the Mongols," chap. 5.

CHAPTER II

ON TO SHEN-SHEN AND THENCE TO KHOTEN

After travelling for seventeen days, a distance we may calculate of about 1500 le, (the pilgrims) reached the kingdom of Shen-shen,[1] a country rugged and hilly, with a thin and barren soil. The clothes of the common people are coarse, and like those worn in our land of Han,[2] some wearing felt and others coarse serge or cloth of hair;-- this was the only difference seen among them. The king professed (our) Law, and there might be in the country more than four thousand monks,[3] who were all students of the hinayana.[4] The common people of this and other kingdoms (in that region), as well as the sramans,[5] all practise the rules of India,[6] only that the latter do so more exactly, and the former more loosely. So (the travellers) found it in all the kingdoms through which they went on their way from this to the west, only that each had its own peculiar barbarous speech.[7] (The monks), however, who had (given up the worldly life) and quitted their families, were all students of Indian books and the Indian language. Here they stayed for about a month, and then proceeded on their journey, fifteen days walking to the north-west bringing them to the country of Woo-e.[8] In this also there were more than four thousand monks, all students of the hinayana. They were very strict in their rules, so that sramans from the

19

territory of Ts'in[9] were all unprepared for their regulations. Fa-hien, through the management of Foo Kung-sun, /maitre d'hotellerie/,[10] was able to remain (with his company in the monastery where they were received) for more than two months, and here they were rejoined by Pao-yun and his friends.[11] (At the end of that time) the people of Woo-e neglected the duties of propriety and righteousness, and treated the strangers in so niggardly a manner that Che-yen, Hwuy-keen, and Hwuy- wei went back towards Kao-ch'ang,[12] hoping to obtain there the means of continuing their journey. Fa-hien and the rest, however, through the liberality of Foo Kung-sun, managed to go straight forward in a south-west direction. They found the country uninhabited as they went along. The difficulties which they encountered in crossing the streams and on their route, and the sufferings which they endured, were unparalleled in human experience, but in the course of a month and five days they succeeded in reaching Yu-teen.[13]

NOTES

[1] An account is given of the kingdom of Shen-shen in the 96th of the Books of the first Han dynasty, down to its becoming a dependency of China, about B.C. 80. The greater portion of that is now accessible to the English reader in a translation by Mr. Wylie in the "Journal of the Anthropological Institute," August, 1880. Mr. Wylie says:-- "Although we may not be able to identify Shen-shen with certainty, yet we have sufficient indications to give an appropriate idea of its position, as being south of and not far from lake Lob." He then goes into an exhibition of those indications, which I need not transcribe. It is sufficient for us to know that the capital city was not far from Lob or Lop Nor, into which in lon. 38d E. the Tarim flows. Fa-hien estimated its distance to be 1500 le from T'un-hwang. He and his companions must have gone more than twenty-five miles a day to accomplish the journey in seventeen days.

[2] This is the name which Fa-hien always uses when he would speak of China, his native country, as a whole, calling it from the great dynasty which had ruled it, first and last, for between four and five centuries. Occasionally, as we shall immediately see, he speaks of "the territory of Ts'in or Ch'in," but

intending thereby only the kingdom or Ts'in, having its capital, as described in the first note on the last chapter, in Ch'ang-gan.

[3] So I prefer to translate the character {.} (sang) rather than by "priests." Even in Christianity, beyond the priestly privilege which belongs to all believers, I object to the ministers of any denomination or church calling themselves or being called "priests;" and much more is the name inapplicable to the sramanas or bhikshus of Buddhism which acknowledges no God in the universe, no soul in man, and has no services of sacrifice or prayer in its worship. The only difficulty in the use of "monks" is caused by the members of the sect in Japan which, since the middle of the fifteenth century, has abolished the prohibition against marrying on the part of its ministers, and other prohibitions in diet and dress. Sang and sang-kea represent the Sanskrit sangha, constituted by at least four members, and empowered to hear confession, to grant absolution, to admit persons to holy orders, &c.; secondly, the third constituent of the Buddhistic Trinity, a deification of the /communio sanctorum/, or the Buddhist order. The name is used by our author of the monks collectively or individually as belonging to the class, and may be considered as synonymous with the name sramana, which will immediately claim our attention.

[4] Meaning the "small vehicle, or conveyance." There are in Buddhism the triyana, or "three different means of salvation, i.e. of conveyance across the samsara, or sea of transmigration, to the shores of nirvana. Afterwards the term was used to designate the different phases of development through which the Buddhist dogma passed, known as the mahayana, hinayana, and madhyamayana." "The hinayana is the simplest vehicle of salvation, corresponding to the first of the three degrees of saintship. Characteristics of it are the preponderance of active moral asceticism, and the absence of speculative mysticism and quietism." E. H., pp. 151-2, 45, and 117.

[5] The name for India is here the same as in the former chapter and throughout the book,--T'een-chuh ({.} {.}), the chuh being pronounced, probably, in Fa-hien's time as tuk. How the earliest name for India, Shin-tuk or duk=Scinde, came to be changed into Thien-tuk, it would take too much space to explain. I believe it was done by the Buddhists, wishing to give a

good auspicious name to the fatherland of their Law, and calling it "the Heavenly Tuk," just as the Mohammedans call Arabia "the Heavenly region" ({.} {.}), and the court of China itself is called "the Celestial" ({.} {.}).

[6] Sraman may in English take the place of Sramana (Pali, Samana; in Chinese, Sha-man), the name for Buddhist monks, as those who have separated themselves from (left) their families, and quieted their hearts from all intrusion of desire and lust. "It is employed, first, as a general name for ascetics of all demoninations, and, secondly, as a general designation of Buddhistic monks." E. H., pp. 130, 131.

[7] Tartar or Mongolian.

[8] Woo-e has not been identified. Watters ("China Review," viii. 115) says:--"We cannot be far wrong if we place it in Kharaschar, or between that and Kutscha." It must have been a country of considerable size to have so many monks in it.

[9] This means in one sense China, but Fa-hien, in his use of the name, was only thinking of the three Ts'in states of which I have spoken in a previous note; perhaps only of that from the capital of which he had himself set out.

[10] This sentence altogether is difficult to construe, and Mr. Watters, in the "China Review," was the first to disentangle more than one knot in it. I am obliged to adopt the reading of {.} {.} in the Chinese editions, instead of the {.} {.} in the Corean text. It seems clear that only one person is spoken of as assisting the travellers, and his name, as appears a few sentences farther on, was Foo Kung-sun. The {.} {.} which immediately follows the surname Foo {.}, must be taken as the name of his office, corresponding, as the {.} shows, to that of /le maitre d'hotellerie/ in a Roman Catholic abbey. I was once indebted myself to the kind help of such an officer at a monastery in Canton province. The Buddhistic name for him is uddesika=overseer. The Kung-sun that follows his surname indicates that he was descended from some feudal lord in the old times of the Chow dynasty. We know indeed of no ruling house which had the surname of Foo, but its adoption by the grandson of a ruler can be satisfactorily accounted for; and his posterity continued to call

themselves Kung-sun, duke or lord's grandson, and so retain the memory of the rank of their ancestor.

[11] Whom they had left behind them at T'un-hwang.

[12] The country of the Ouighurs, the district around the modern Turfan or Tangut.

[13] Yu-teen is better known as Khoten. Dr. P. Smith gives (p. 11) the following description of it:--"A large district on the south-west of the desert of Gobi, embracing all the country south of Oksu and Yarkand, along the northern base of the Kwun-lun mountains, for more than 300 miles from east to west. The town of the same name, now called Ilchi, is in an extensive plain on the Khoten river, in lat. 37d N., and lon. 80d 35s E. After the Tungani insurrection against Chinese rule in 1862, the Mufti Haji Habeeboolla was made governor of Khoten, and held the office till he was murdered by Yakoob Beg, who became for a time the conqueror of all Chinese Turkestan. Khoten produces fine linen and cotton stuffs, jade ornaments, copper, grain, and fruits." The name in Sanskrit is Kustana. (E. H., p. 60).

CHAPTER III

KHOTEN. PROCESSIONS OF IMAGES. THE KING'S NEW MONASTERY.

Yu-teen is a pleasant and prosperous kingdom, with a numerous and flourishing population. The inhabitants all profess our Law, and join together in its religious music for their enjoyment.[1] The monks amount to several myriads, most of whom are students of the mahayana.[2] They all receive their food from the common store.[3] Throughout the country the houses of the people stand apart like (separate) stars, and each family has a small tope[4] reared in front of its door. The smallest of these may be twenty cubits high, or rather more.[5] They make (in the monasteries) rooms for monks from all quarters,[5] the use of which is given to travelling monks who may arrive, and who are provided with whatever else they require.

The lord of the country lodged Fa-hien and the others comfortably, and supplied their wants, in a monastery[6] called Gomati,[6] of the mahayana school. Attached to it there are three thousand monks, who are called to their meals by the sound of a bell. When they enter the refectory, their demeanour is marked by a reverent gravity, and they take their seats in regular order, all maintaining a perfect silence. No sound is heard from their alms-bowls and other utensils. When any of these pure men[7] require food, they are not allowed to call out (to the attendants) for it, but only make signs with their hands.

Hwuy-king, Tao-ching, and Hwuy-tah set out in advance towards the country of K'eeh-ch'a;[8] but Fa-hien and the others, wishing to see the procession of images, remained behind for three months. There are in this country four[9] great monasteries, not counting the smaller ones. Beginning on the first day of the fourth month, they sweep and water the streets inside the city, making a grand display in the lanes and byways. Over the city gate they pitch a large tent, grandly adorned in all possible ways, in which the king and queen, with their ladies brilliantly arrayed,[10] take up their residence (for the time).

The monks of the Gomati monastery, being mahayana students, and held in great reverence by the king, took precedence of all others in the procession. At a distance of three or four le from the city, they made a four-wheeled image car, more than thirty cubits high, which looked like the great hall (of a monastery) moving along. The seven precious substances[11] were grandly displayed about it, with silken streamers and canopies hanging all around. The (chief) image[12] stood in the middle of the car, with two Bodhisattvas[13] in attendance upon it, while devas[14] were made to follow in waiting, all brilliantly carved in gold and silver, and hanging in the air. When (the car) was a hundred paces from the gate, the king put off his crown of state, changed his dress for a fresh suit, and with bare feet, carrying in his hands flowers and incense, and with two rows of attending followers, went out at the gate to meet the image; and, with his head and face (bowed to the ground), he did homage at its feet, and then scattered the flowers and burnt the incense. When the image was entering the gate, the queen and the brilliant ladies with her in the gallery above scattered far and wide all kinds of flowers, which floated about and fell promiscuously to the ground. In this way everything was done to promote the dignity of the occasion. The carriages of the monasteries were all different, and each one had its own day for the procession. (The ceremony) began on the first day of the fourth month, and ended on the fourteenth, after which the king and queen returned to the palace.

Seven or eight le to the west of the city there is what is called the King's New Monastery, the building of which took eighty years, and extended over three reigns. It may be 250 cubits in height, rich in elegant carving and inlaid work, covered above with gold and silver, and finished throughout with a combination of all the precious substances. Behind the tope there has been built a Hall of Buddha,[15] of the utmost magnificence and beauty, the beams, pillars, venetianed doors, and windows being all overlaid with gold-leaf. Besides this, the apartments for the monks are imposingly and elegantly decorated, beyond the power of words to express. Of whatever things of highest value and preciousness the kings in the six countries on the east of the (Ts'ung) range of mountains[16] are possessed, they contribute the greater portion (to this monastery), using but a small portion of them themselves.[17]

NOTES

[1] This fondness for music among the Khoteners is mentioned by Hsuan and Ch'wang and others.

[2] Mahayana. It is a later form of the Buddhist doctrine, the second phase of its development corresponding to the state of a Bodhisattva, who, being able to transport himself and all mankind to nirvana, may be compared to a huge vehicle. See Davids on the "Key-note of the 'Great Vehicle,'" Hibbert Lectures, p. 254.

[3] Fa-hien supplies sufficient information of how the common store or funds of the monasteries were provided, farther on in chapters xvi and xxxix, as well as in other passages. As the point is important, I will give here, from

Davids' fifth Hibbert Lecture (p. 178), some of the words of the dying Buddha, taken from "The Book of the Great Decease," as illustrating the statement in this text:--"So long as the brethren shall persevere in kindness of action, speech, and thought among the saints, both in public and private; so long as they shall divide without partiality, and share in common with the upright and holy, all such things as they receive in accordance with the just provisions of the order, down even to the mere contents of a begging bowl; . . . so long may the brethren be expected not to decline, but to prosper."

[4] The Chinese {.} (t'ah; in Cantonese, t'ap), as used by Fa-hien, is, no doubt, a phonetisation of the Sanskrit stupa or Pali thupa; and it is well in translating to use for the structures described by him the name of topes,--made familiar by Cunningham and other Indian antiquarians. In the thirteenth chapter there is an account of one built under the superintendence of Buddha himself, "as a model for all topes in future." They were usually in the form of bell-shaped domes, and were solid, surmounted by a long tapering pinnacle formed with a series of rings, varying in number. But their form, I suppose, was often varied; just as we have in China pagodas of different shapes. There are several topes now in the Indian Institute at Oxford, brought from Buddha Gaya, but the largest of them is much smaller than "the smallest" of those of Khoten. They were intended chiefly to contain the relics of Buddha and famous masters of his Law; but what relics could there be in the Tiratna topes of chapter xvi?

[5] The meaning here is much disputed. The author does not mean to say that the monk's apartments were made "square," but that the monasteries were made with many guest-chambers or spare rooms.

[6] The Sanskrit term for a monastery is used here,--Sangharama, "gardens of the assembly," originally denoting only "the surrounding park, but afterwards transferred to the whole of the premises" (E. H., p. 118). Gomati, the name of this monastery, means "rich in cows."

[7] A denomination for the monks as vimala, "undefiled" or "pure." Giles makes it "the menials that attend on the monks," but I have not met with it in

26

that application.

[8] K'eeh-ch'a has not been clearly identified. Remusat made it Cashmere; Klaproth, Iskardu; Beal makes it Kartchou; and Eitel, Khas'a, "an ancient tribe on the Paropamisus, the Kasioi of Ptolemy." I think it was Ladak, or some well-known place in it. Hwuy-tah, unless that name be an alias, appears here for the first time.

[9] Instead of "four," the Chinese copies of the text have "fourteen;" but the Corean reading is, probably, more correct.

[10] There may have been, as Giles says, "maids of honour;" but the character does not say so.

[11] The Sapta-ratna, gold, silver, lapis lazuli, rock crystal, rubies, diamonds or emeralds, and agate. See Sacred Books of the East (Davids' Buddhist Suttas), vol. xi., p. 249.

[12] No doubt that of Sakyamuni himself.

[13] A Bodhisattva is one whose essence has become intelligence; a Being who will in some future birth as a man (not necessarily or usually the next) attain to Buddhahood. The name does not include those Buddhas who have not yet attained to pari-nirvana. The symbol of the state is an elephant fording a river. Popularly, its abbreviated form P'u-sa is used in China for any idol or image; here the name has its proper signification.

[14] {.} {.}, "all the thien," or simply "the thien" taken as plural. But in Chinese the character called thien {.} denotes heaven, or Heaven, and is interchanged with Ti and Shang Ti, meaning God. With the Buddhists it denotes the devas or Brahmanic gods, or all the inhabitants of the six devalokas. The usage shows the antagonism between Buddhism and Brahmanism, and still more that between it and Confucianism.

[15] Giles and Williams call this "the oratory of Buddha." But "oratory" gives the idea of a small apartment, whereas the name here leads the mind to

think of a large "hall." I once accompanied the monks of a large monastery from their refectory to the Hall of Buddha, which was a lofty and spacious apartment splendidly fitted up.

[16] The Ts'ung, or "Onion" range, called also the Belurtagh mountains, including the Karakorum, and forming together the connecting links between the more northern T'een-shan and the Kwun-lun mountains on the north of Thibet. It would be difficult to name the six countries which Fa-hien had in mind.

[17] This seems to be the meaning here. My first impression of it was that the author meant to say that the contributions which they received were spent by the monks mainly on the buildings, and only to a small extent for themselves; and I still hesitate between that view and the one in the version.

There occurs here the binomial phrase kung-yang {.} {.}, which is one of the most common throughout the narrative, and is used not only of support in the way of substantial contributions given to monks, monasteries, and Buddhism, but generally of all Buddhistic worship, if I may use that term in the connexion. Let me here quote two or three sentences from Davids' Manual (pp. 168-170):--"The members of the order are secured from want. There is no place in the Buddhist scheme for churches; the offering of flowers before the sacred tree or image of the Buddha takes the place of worship. Buddhism does not acknowledge the efficacy of prayers; and in the warm countries where Buddhists live, the occasional reading of the law, or preaching of the word, in public, can take place best in the open air, by moonlight, under a simple roof of trees or palms. There are five principal kinds of meditation, which in Buddhism takes the place of prayer."

CHAPTER IV

THROUGH THE TS'UNG OR "ONION" MOUNTAINS TO K'EEH-CH'A;--PROBABLY SKARDO, OR SOME CITY MORE TO THE EAST IN LADAK

When the processions of images in the fourth month were over, Sang- shao, by himself alone, followed a Tartar who was an earnest follower of the Law,[1] and proceeded towards Kophene.[2] Fa-hien and the others went forward to the kingdom of Tsze-hoh, which it took them twenty-five days to reach.[3] Its king was a strenuous follower of our Law,[4] and had (around him) more than a thousand monks, mostly students of the mahayana. Here (the travellers) abode fifteen days, and then went south for four days, when they found themselves among the Ts'ung-ling mountains, and reached the country of Yu-hwuy,[5] where they halted and kept their retreat.[6] When this was over, they went on among the hills[7] for twenty-five days, and got to K'eeh- ch'a,[8] there rejoining Hwuy-king[9] and his two companions.

NOTES

[1] This Tartar is called a {.} {.}, "a man of the Tao," or faith of Buddha. It occurs several times in the sequel, and denotes the man who is not a Buddhist outwardly only, but inwardly as well, whose faith is always making itself manifest in his ways. The name may be used of followers of other systems of faith besides Buddhism.

[2] See the account of the kingdom of Kophene, in the 96th Book of the first Han Records, p. 78, where its capital is said to be 12,200 le from Ch'ang-gan. It was the whole or part of the present Cabulistan. The name of Cophene is connected with the river Kophes, supposed to be the same as the present Cabul river, which falls into the Indus, from the west, at Attock, after passing Peshawar. The city of Cabul, the capital of Afghanistan, may be the Kophene of the text; but we do not know that Sang-shao and his guide got so far west. The text only says that they set out from Khoten "towards it."

[3] Tsze-hoh has not been identified. Beal thinks it was Yarkand, which, however, was north-west from Khoten. Watters ("China Review," p. 135) rather approves the suggestion of "Tashkurgan in Sirikul" for it. As it took Fa-hien twenty-five days to reach it, it must have been at least 150 miles from Khoten.

[4] The king is described here by a Buddhistic phrase, denoting the possession of viryabala, "the power of energy; persevering exertion-- one of

the five moral powers" (E. H., p. 170).

[5] Nor has Yu-hwuy been clearly identified. Evidently it was directly south from Tsze-hoh, and among the "Onion" mountains. Watters hazards the conjecture that it was the Aktasch of our present maps.

[6] This was the retreat already twice mentioned as kept by the pilgrims in the summer, the different phraseology, "quiet rest," without any mention of the season, indicating their approach to India, E. H., p. 168. Two, if not three, years had elapsed since they left Ch'ang-gan. Are we now with them in 402?

[7] This is the Corean reading {.}, much preferable to the {.} of the Chinese editions.

[8] Watters approves of Klaproth's determination of K'eeh-ch'a to be Iskardu or Skardo. There are difficulties in connexion with the view, but it has the advantage, to my mind very great, of bringing the pilgrims across the Indus. The passage might be accomplished with ease at this point of the river's course, and therefore is not particularly mentioned.

[9] Who had preceded them from Khoten.

CHAPTER V

GREAT QUINQUENNIAL ASSEMBLY OF MONKS. RELICS OF BUDDHA. PRODUCTIONS OF THE COUNTRY.

It happened that the king of the country was then holding the pancha parishad, that is, in Chinese, the great quinquennial assembly.[1] When this is to be held, the king requests the presence of the Sramans from all quarters (of his kingdom). They come (as if) in clouds; and when they are all assembled, their place of session is grandly decorated. Silken streamers and canopies are hung out in, and water- lilies in gold and silver are made and fixed up behind the places where (the chief of them) are to sit. When clean mats have been spread, and they are all seated, the king and his ministers present their offerings according to rule and law. (The assembly takes place), in the first, second, or third month, for the most part in the spring.

After the king has held the assembly, he further exhorts the ministers to make other and special offerings. The doing of this extends over one, two, three, five, or even seven days; and when all is finished, he takes his own riding-horse, saddles, bridles, and waits on him himself,[2] while he makes the noblest and most important minister of the kingdom mount him. Then, taking fine white woollen cloth, all sorts of precious things, and articles which the Sramans require, he distributes them among them, uttering vows at the same time along with all his ministers; and when this distribution has taken place, he again redeems (whatever he wishes) from the monks.[3]

The country, being among the hills and cold, does not produce the other cereals, and only the wheat gets ripe. After the monks have received their annual (portion of this), the mornings suddenly show the hoar-frost, and on this account the king always begs the monks to make the wheat ripen[4] before they receive their portion. There is in the country a spitoon which belonged to Buddha, made of stone, and in colour like his alms-bowl. There is also a tooth of Buddha, for which the people have reared a tope, connected with which there are more than a thousand monks and their disciples,[5] all students of the hinayana. To the east of these hills the dress of the common people is of coarse materials, as in our country of Ts'in, but here also[6] there were among them the differences of fine woollen cloth and of serge or haircloth. The rules observed by the Sramans are remarkable, and too numerous to be mentioned in detail. The country is in the midst of the Onion range. As you go forward from these mountains, the plants, trees, and fruits are all different from those of the land of Han, excepting only the bamboo, pomegranate,[7] and sugar-cane.

NOTES

[1] See Eitel, p. 89. He describes the assembly as "an ecclesiastical conference, first instituted by king Asoka for general confession of sins and inculcation of morality."

[2] The text of this sentence is perplexing; and all translators, including

31

myself, have been puzzled by it.

[3] See what we are told of king Asoka's grant of all the Jambudvipa to the monks in chapter xxvii. There are several other instances of similar gifts in the Mahavansa.

[4] Watters calls attention to this as showing that the monks of K'eeh-ch'a had the credit of possessing weather-controlling powers.

[5] The text here has {.} {.}, not {.} alone. I often found in monasteries boys and lads who looked up to certain of the monks as their preceptors.

[6] Compare what is said in chapter ii of the dress of the people of Shen-shen.

[7] Giles thinks the fruit here was the guava, because the ordinary name for "pomegranate" is preceded by gan {.}; but the pomegranate was called at first Gan Shih-lau, as having been introduced into China from Gan-seih by Chang-k'een, who is referred to in chapter vii.

CHAPTER VI

ON TOWARDS NORTH INDIA. DARADA. IMAGE OF MAITREYA BODHISATTVA.

From this (the travellers) went westwards towards North India, and after being on the way for a month, they succeeded in getting across and through the range of the Onion mountains. The snow rests on them both winter and summer. There are also among them venomous dragons, which, when provoked, spit forth poisonous winds, and cause showers of snow and storms of sand and gravel. Not one in ten thousand of those who encounter these dangers escapes with his life. The people of the country call the range by the name of "The Snow mountains." When (the travellers) had got through them, they were in North India, and immediately on entering its borders, found themselves in a small kingdom called T'o-leih,[1] where also there were many monks, all students of the hinayana.

In this kingdom there was formerly an Arhan,[2] who by his supernatural power[3] took a clever artificer up to the Tushita heaven, to see the height, complexion, and appearance of Maitreya Bodhisattva,[4] and then return and make an image of him in wood. First and last, this was done three times, and then the image was completed, eighty cubits in height, and eight cubits at the base from knee to knee of the crossed legs. On fast-days it emits an effulgent light. The kings of the (surrounding) countries vie with one another in presenting offerings to it. Here it is,--to be seen now as of old.[5]

NOTES

[1] Eitel and others identify this with Darada, the country of the ancient Dardae, the region near Dardus; lat. 30d 11s N., lon. 73d 54s E. See E. H. p. 30. I am myself in more than doubt on the point. Cunningham ("Ancient Geography of India," p. 82) says "Darel is a valley on the right or western bank of the Indus, now occupied by Dardus or Dards, from whom it received its name." But as I read our narrative, Fa-hien is here on the eastern bank of the Indus, and only crosses to the western bank as described in the next chapter.

[2] Lo-han, Arhat, Arahat, are all designations of the perfected Arya, the disciple who has passed the different stages of the Noble Path, or eightfold excellent way, who has conquered all passions, and is not to be reborn again. Arhatship implies possession of certain supernatural powers, and is not to be succeeded by Buddhaship, but implies the fact of the saint having already attained nirvana. Popularly, the Chinese designate by this name the wider circle of Buddha's disciples, as well as the smaller ones of 500 and 18. No temple in Canton is better worth a visit than that of the 500 Lo-han.

[3] Riddhi-sakshatkriya, "the power of supernatural footsteps,"="a body flexible at pleasure," or unlimited power over the body. E. H., p. 104.

[4] Tushita is the fourth Devaloka, where all Bodhisattvas are reborn before finally appearing on earth as Buddha. Life lasts in Tushita 4000 years, but twenty-four hours there are equal to 400 years on earth. E. H., p. 152.

[5] Maitreya (Spence Hardy, Maitri), often styled Ajita, "the Invincible," was a Bodhisattva, the principal one, indeed, of Sakyamuni's retinue, but is not counted among the ordinary (historical) disciples, nor is anything told of his antecedents. It was in the Tushita heaven that Sakyamuni met him and appointed him as his successor, to appear as Buddha after the lapse of 5000 years. Maitreya is therefore the expected Messiah of the Buddhists, residing at present in Tushita, and, according to the account of him in Eitel (H., p. 70), "already controlling the propagation of the Buddhistic faith." The name means "gentleness" or "kindness;" and this will be the character of his dispensation.

[6] The combination of {.} {.} in the text of this concluding sentence, and so frequently occurring throughout the narrative, has occasioned no little dispute among previous translators. In the imperial thesaurus of phraseology (P'ei-wan Yun-foo), under {.}, an example of it is given from Chwang-tsze, and a note subjoined that {.} {.} is equivalent to {.} {.}, "anciently and now."

CHAPTER VII

CROSSING OF THE INDUS. WHEN BUDDHISM FIRST CROSSED THE RIVER FOR THE EAST

The travellers went on to the south-west for fifteen days (at the foot of the mountains, and) following the course of their range. The way was difficult and rugged, (running along) a bank exceedingly precipitous, which rose up there, a hill-like wall of rock, 10,000 cubits from the base. When one approaches the edge of it, his eyes become unsteady; and if he wished to go forward in the same direction, there was no place on which he could place his foot; and beneath where the waters of the river called the Indus.[1] In former times men had chiselled paths along the rocks, and distributed ladders on the face of them, to the number altogether of 700, at the bottom of which there was a suspension bridge of ropes, by which the river was crossed, its banks being there eighty paces apart.[2] The (place and arrangements) are to be found in the Records of the Nine Interpreters,[3] but neither Chang K'een[4] nor Kan Ying[5] had reached the spot.

The monks[6] asked Fa-hien if it could be known when the Law of Buddha first went to the east. He replied, "When I asked the people of those countries about it, they all said that it had been handed down by their fathers from of old that, after the setting up of the image of Maitreya Bodhisattva, there were Sramans of India who crossed this river, carrying with them Sutras and Books of Discipline. Now the image was set up rather more than 300 years after the nirvana[7] of Buddha, which may be referred to the reign of king P'ing of the Chow dynasty.[8] According to this account we may say that the diffusion of our great doctrines (in the east) began from (the setting up of) this image. If it had not been through that Maitreya,[9] the great spiritual master[10] (who is to be) the successor of the Sakya, who could have caused the 'Three Precious Ones'[11] to be proclaimed so far, and the people of those border lands to know our Law? We know of a truth that the opening of (the way for such) a mysterious propagation is not the work of man; and so the dream of the emperor Ming of Han[12] had its proper cause."

NOTES

[1] The Sindhu. We saw in a former note that the earliest name in China for India was Shin-tuh. So, here, the river Indus is called by a name approaching that in sound.

[2] Both Beal and Watters quote from Cunningham (Ladak, pp. 88, 89) the following description of the course of the Indus in these parts, in striking accordance with our author's account:--"From Skardo to Rongdo, and from Rongdo to Makpou-i-shang-rong, for upwards of 100 miles, the Indus sweeps sullen and dark through a mighty gorge in the mountains, which for wild sublimity is perhaps unequalled. Rongdo means the country of defiles. . . . Between these points the Indus raves from side to side of the gloomy chasm, foaming and chafing with ungovernable fury. Yet even in these inaccessible places has daring and ingenious man triumphed over opposing nature. The yawning abyss is spanned by frail rope bridges, and the narrow ledges of rocks are connected by ladders to form a giddy pathway

overhanging the seething cauldron below."

[3] The Japanese edition has a different reading here from the Chinese copies,--one which Remusat (with true critical instinct) conjectured should take the place of the more difficult text with which alone he was acquainted. The "Nine Interpreters" would be a general name for the official interpreters attached to the invading armies of Han in their attempts to penetrate and subdue the regions of the west. The phrase occurs in the memoir of Chang K'een, referred to in the next note.

[4] Chang K'een, a minister of the emperor Woo of Han (B.C. 140-87), is celebrated as the first Chinese who "pierced the void," and penetrated to "the regions of the west," corresponding very much to the present Turkestan. Through him, by B.C. 115, a regular intercourse was established between China and the thirty-six kingdoms or states of that quarter;--see Mayers' Chinese Reader's Manual, p. 5. The memoir of Chang K'een, translated by Mr. Wylie from the Books of the first Han dynasty, appears in the Journal of the Anthropological Institute, referred to already.

[5] Less is known of Kan Ying than of Chang K'een. Being sent in A.D. 88 by his patron Pan Chao on an embassy to the Roman empire, he only got as far as the Caspian sea, and returned to China. He extended, however, the knowledge of his countrymen with regard to the western regions;--see the memoir of Pan Chao in the Books of the second Han, and Mayers' Manual, pp. 167, 168.

[6] Where and when? Probably at his first resting-place after crossing the Indus.

[7] This may refer to Sakyamuni's becoming Buddha on attaining to nirvana, or more probably to his pari-nirvana and death.

[8] As king P'ing's reign lasted from B.C. 750 to 719, this would place the death of Buddha in the eleventh century B.C., whereas recent inquirers place it between B.C. 480 and 470, a year or two, or a few years, after that of Confucius, so that the two great "Masters" of the east were really

contemporaries. But if Rhys Davids be correct, as I think he is, in fixing the date of Buddha's death within a few years of 412 B.C. (see Manual, p. 213), not to speak of Westergaard's still lower date, then the Buddha was very considerably the junior of Confucius.

[9] This confirms the words of Eitel, that Maitreya is already controlling the propagation of the faith.

[10] The Chinese characters for this simply mean "the great scholar or officer;" but see Eitel's Handbook, p. 99, on the term purusha.

[11] "The precious Buddha," "the precious Law," and "the precious Monkhood;" Buddha, Dharma, and Sangha; the whole being equivalent to Buddhism.

[12] Fa-hien thus endorses the view that Buddhism was introduced into China in this reign, A.D. 58-75. The emperor had his dream in A.D. 61.

CHAPTER VIII

WOO-CHANG, OR UDYANA. MONASTERIES, AND THEIR WAYS. TRACES OF BUDDHA.

After crossing the river, (the travellers) immediately came to the kingdom of Woo-chang,[1] which is indeed (a part) of North India. The people all use the language of Central India, "Central India" being what we should call the "Middle Kingdom." The food and clothes of the common people are the same as in that Central Kingdom. The Law of Buddha is very (flourishing in Woo-chang). They call the places where the monks stay (for a time) or reside permanently Sangharamas; and of these there are in all 500, the monks being all students of the hinayana. When stranger bhikshus[2] arrive at one of them, their wants are supplied for three days, after which they are told to find a resting-place for themselves.

There is a tradition that when Buddha came to North India, he came at once to this country, and that here he left a print of his foot, which is long or short according to the ideas of the beholder (on the subject). It exists, and the same thing is true about it, at the present day. Here also are still to be seen the rock on which he dried his clothes, and the place where he converted the wicked dragon.[3] The rock is fourteen cubits high, and more than twenty broad, with one side of it smooth.

Hwuy-king, Hwuy-tah, and Tao-ching went on ahead towards (the place of) Buddha's shadow in the country of Nagara;[4] but Fa-hien and the others remained in Woo-chang, and kept the summer retreat.[5] That over, they descended south, and arrived in the country of Soo-ho-to.[6]

NOTES

[1] Udyana, meaning "the Park;" just north of the Punjab, the country along the Subhavastu, now called the Swat; noted for its forests, flowers, and fruits (E. H., p. 153).

[2] Bhikshu is the name for a monk as "living by alms," a mendicant. All bhikshus call themselves Sramans. Sometimes the two names are used together by our author.

[3] Naga is the Sanskrit name for the Chinese lung or dragon; often meaning a snake, especially the boa. "Chinese Buddhists," says Eitel, p. 79, "when speaking of nagas as boa spirits, always represent them as enemies of mankind, but when viewing them as deities of rivers, lakes, or oceans, they describe them as piously inclined." The dragon, however, is in China the symbol of the Sovereign and Sage, a use of it unknown in Buddhism, according to which all nagas need to be converted in order to obtain a higher phase of being. The use of the character too {.}, as here, in the sense of "to convert," is entirely Buddhistic. The six paramitas are the six virtues which carry men across {.} the great sea of life and death, as the sphere of transmigration to nirvana. With regard to the particular conversion here, Eitel (p. 11) says the Naga's name was Apatala, the guardian deity of the Subhavastu river, and that he was converted by Sakyamuni shortly before the death of the latter.

[4] In Chinese Na-k'eeh, an ancient kingdom and city on the southern bank of the Cabul river, about thirty miles west of Jellalabad.

[5] We would seem now to be in 403.

[6] Soo-ho-to has not been clearly identified. Beal says that later Buddhist writers include it in Udyana. It must have been between the Indus and the Swat. I suppose it was what we now call Swastene.

CHAPTER IX

SOO-HO-TO. LEGEND OF BUDDHA.

In that country also Buddhism[1] is flourishing. There is in it the place where Sakra,[2] Ruler of Devas, in a former age,[3] tried the Bodhisattva, by producing[4] a hawk (in pursuit of a) dove, when (the Bodhisattva) cut off a piece of his own flesh, and (with it) ransomed the dove. After Buddha had attained to perfect wisdom,[5] and in travelling about with his disciples (arrived at this spot), he informed them that this was the place where he ransomed the dove with a piece of his own flesh. In this way the people of the country became aware of the fact, and on the spot reared a tope, adorned with layers[6] of gold and silver plates.

NOTES

[1] Buddhism stands for the two Chinese characters {.} {.}, "the Law of Buddha," and to that rendering of the phrase, which is of frequent occurrence, I will in general adhere. Buddhism is not an adequate rendering of them any more than Christianity would be of {to euaggelion Xristou}. The Fa or Law is the equivalent of dharma comprehending all in the first Basket of the Buddhist teaching,--as Dr. Davids says (Hibbert Lectures, p. 44), "its ethics and philosophy, and its system of self-culture;" with the theory of karma, it seems to me, especially underlying it. It has been pointed out (Cunningham's "Bhilsa Topes," p. 102) that dharma is the keystone of all king Priyadarsi or Asoka's edicts. The whole of them are dedicated to the attainment of one object, "the advancement of dharma, or of the Law of

Buddha." His native Chinese afforded no better character than {.} or Law, by which our author could express concisely his idea of the Buddhistic system, as "a law of life," a directory or system of Rules, by which men could attain to the consummation of their being.

[2] Sakra is a common name for the Brahmanic Indra, adopted by Buddhism into the circle of its own great adherents;--it has been said, "because of his popularity." He is generally styled, as here, T'een Ti, "God or Ruler of Devas." He is now the representative of the secular power, the valiant protector of the Buddhist body, but is looked upon as inferior to Sakyamuni, and every Buddhist saint. He appears several times in Fa-hien's narrative. E. H., pp. 108 and 46.

[3] The Chinese character is {.}, "formerly," and is often, as in the first sentence of the narrative, simply equivalent to that adverb. At other times it means, as here, "in a former age," some pre-existent state in the time of a former birth. The incident related is "a Jataka story."

[4] It occurs at once to the translator to render the characters {.} {.} by "changed himself to." Such is often their meaning in the sequel, but their use in chapter xxiv may be considered as a crucial test of the meaning which I have given them here.

[5] That is, had become Buddha, or completed his course {.} {.}.

[6] This seems to be the contribution of {.} (or {.}), to the force of the binomial {.} {.}, which is continually occurring.

CHAPTER X

GANDHARA. LEGENDS OF BUDDHA.

The travellers, going downwards from this towards the east, in five days came to the country of Gandhara,[1] the place where Dharma- vivardhana,[2] the son of Asoka,[3] ruled. When Buddha was a Bodhisattva, he gave his eyes also for another man here;[4] and at the spot they have also reared a large tope, adorned with layers of gold and silver plates. The people of the country were mostly students of the hinayana.

NOTES

[1] Eitel says "an ancient kingdom, corresponding to the region about Dheri and Banjour." But see note 5.

[2] Dharma-vivardhana is the name in Sanskrit, represented by the Fa Yi {.} {.} of the text.

[3] Asoka is here mentioned for the first time;--the Constantine of the Buddhist society, and famous for the number of viharas and topes which he erected. He was the grandson of Chandragupta (i.q. Sandracottus), a rude adventurer, who at one time was a refugee in the camp of Alexander the Great; and within about twenty years afterwards drove the Greeks out of India, having defeated Seleucus, the Greek ruler of the Indus provinces. He had by that time made himself king of Magadha. His grandson was converted to Buddhism by the bold and patient demeanour of an Arhat whom he had ordered to be buried alive, and became a most zealous supporter of the new faith. Dr. Rhys Davids (Sacred Books of the East, vol. xi, p. xlvi) says that "Asoka's coronation can be fixed with absolute certainty within a year or two either way of 267 B.C."

[4] This also is a Jataka story; but Eitel thinks it may be a myth, constructed from the story of the blinding of Dharma-vivardhana.

CHAPTER XI

TAKSHASILA. LEGENDS. THE FOUR GREAT TOPES.

Seven days' journey from this to the east brought the travellers to the kingdom of Takshasila,[1] which means "the severed head" in the language of China. Here, when Buddha was a Bodhisattva, he gave away his head to a man;[2] and from this circumstance the kingdom got its name.

Going on further for two days to the east, they came to the place where the

Bodhisattva threw down his body to feed a starving tigress.[2] In these two places also large topes have been built, both adorned with layers of all the precious substances. The kings, ministers, and peoples of the kingdoms around vie with one another in making offerings at them. The trains of those who come to scatter flowers and light lamps at them never cease. The nations of those quarters all those (and the other two mentioned before) "the four great topes."

NOTES

[1] See Julien's "Methode pour dechiffrer et transcrire les Nomes Sanscrits," p. 206. Eitel says, "The Taxila of the Greeks, the region near Hoosun Abdaul in lat. 35d 48s N., lon. 72d 44s E. But this identification, I am satisfied, is wrong. Cunningham, indeed, takes credit ("Ancient Geography of India," pp. 108, 109) for determining this to be the site of Arrian's Taxila,--in the upper Punjab, still existing in the ruins of Shahdheri, between the Indus and Hydaspes (the modern Jhelum). So far he may be correct; but the Takshasila of Fa-hien was on the other, or western side of the Indus; and between the river and Gandhara. It took him, indeed, seven days travelling eastwards to reach it; but we do not know what stoppages he may have made on the way. We must be wary in reckoning distances from his specifications of days.

[2] Two Jataka stories. See the account of the latter in Spence Hardy's "Manual of Buddhism," pp. 91, 92. It took place when Buddha had been born as a Brahman in the village of Daliddi; and from the merit of the act, he was next born in a devaloka.

CHAPTER XII

PURUSHAPURA, OR PESHAWUR. PROPHECY ABOUT KING KANISHKA AND HIS TOPE. BUDDHA'S ALMS-BOWL. DEATH OF HWUY-YING.

Going southwards from Gandhara, (the travellers) in four days arrived at the kingdom of Purushapura.[1] Formerly, when Buddha was travelling in this country with his disciples, he said to Ananda,[2] "After my pari-nirvana,[3] there will be a king named Kanishka,[4] who shall on this spot build a tope." This Kanishka was afterwards born into the world; and (once), when he had gone forth to look about him, Sakra, Ruler of Devas, wishing to excite the idea in his mind, assumed the appearance of a little herd-boy, and was making a tope right in the way (of the king), who asked what sort of thing he was making. The boy said, "I am making a tope for Buddha." The king said, "Very good;" and immediately, right over the boy's tope, he (proceeded to) rear another, which was more than four hundred cubits high, and adorned with layers of all the precious substances. Of all the topes and temples which (the travellers) saw in their journeyings, there was not one comparable to this in solemn beauty and majestic grandeur. There is a current saying that this is the finest tope in Jambudvipa.[5] When the king's tope was completed, the little tope (of the boy) came out from its side on the south, rather more than three cubits in height.

Buddha's alms-bowl is in this country. Formerly, a king of Yueh-she[6] raised a large force and invaded this country, wishing to carry the bowl away. Having subdued the kingdom, as he and his captains were sincere believers in the Law of Buddha, and wished to carry off the bowl, they proceeded to present their offerings on a great scale. When they had done so to the Three Precious Ones, he made a large elephant be grandly caparisoned, and placed the bowl upon it. But the elephant knelt down on the ground, and was unable to go forward. Again he caused a four-wheeled waggon to be prepared in which the bowl was put to be conveyed away. Eight elephants were then yoked to it, and dragged it with their united strength; but neither were they able to go forward. The king knew that the time for an association between himself and the bowl had not yet arrived,[7] and was sad and deeply ashamed of himself. Forthwith he built a tope at the place and a monastery, and left a guard to watch (the bowl), making all sorts of contributions.

There may be there more than seven hundred monks. When it is near midday, they bring out the bowl, and, along with the common people,[8] make their various offerings to it, after which they take their midday meal. In the evening, at the time of incense, they bring the bowl out again.[9] It may contain rather more than two pecks, and is of various colours, black

43

predominating, with the seams that show its fourfold composition distinctly marked.[10] Its thickness is about the fifth of an inch, and it has a bright and glossy lustre. When poor people throw into it a few flowers, it becomes immediately full, while some very rich people, wishing to make offering of many flowers, might not stop till they had thrown in hundreds, thousands, and myriads of bushels, and yet would not be able to fill it.[11]

Pao-yun and Sang-king here merely made their offerings to the alms- bowl, and (then resolved to) go back. Hwuy-king, Hwuy-tah, and Tao- ching had gone on before the rest to Negara,[12] to make their offerings at (the places of) Buddha's shadow, tooth, and the flat-bone of his skull. (There) Hwuy-king fell ill, and Tao-ching remained to look after him, while Hwuy-tah came alone to Purushapura, and saw the others, and (then) he with Pao-yun and Sang-king took their way back to the land of Ts'in. Hwuy-king[13] came to his end[14] in the monastery of Buddha's alms-bowl, and on this Fa-hien went forward alone towards the place of the flat-bone of Buddha's skull.

NOTES

[1] The modern Peshawur, lat. 34d 8s N., lon. 71d 30s E.

[2] A first cousin of Sakyamuni, and born at the moment when he attained to Buddhaship. Under Buddha's teaching, Ananda became an Arhat, and is famous for his strong and accurate memory; and he played an important part at the first council for the formation of the Buddhist canon. The friendship between Sakyamuni and Ananda was very close and tender; and it is impossible to read much of what the dying Buddha said to him and of him, as related in the Maha-pari-nirvana Sutra, without being moved almost to tears. Ananda is to reappear on earth as Buddha in another Kalpa. See E. H., p. 9, and the Sacred Books of the East, vol. xi.

[3] On his attaining to nirvana, Sakyamuni became the Buddha, and had no longer to mourn his being within the circle of transmigration, and could rejoice in an absolute freedom from passion, and a perfect purity. Still he continued to live on for forty-five years, till he attained to pari-nirvana, and

had done with all the life of sense and society, and had no more exercise of thought. He died; but whether he absolutely and entirely /ceased/ to be, in any sense of the word /being/, it would be difficult to say. Probably he himself would not and could not have spoken definitely on the point. So far as our use of language is concerned, apart from any assured faith in and hope of immortality, his pari-nirvana was his death.

[4] Kanishka appeared, and began to reign, early in our first century, about A.D. 10. He was the last of three brothers, whose original seat was in Yueh-she, immediately mentioned, or Tukhara. Converted by the sudden appearance of a saint, he became a zealous Buddhist, and patronised the system as liberally as Asoka had done. The finest topes in the north-west of India are ascribed to him; he was certainly a great man and a magnificent sovereign.

[5] Jambudvipa is one of the four great continents of the universe, representing the inhabited world as fancied by the Buddhists, and so called because it resembles in shape the leaves of the jambu tree. It is south of mount Meru, and divided among four fabulous kings (E. H., p. 36). It is often used, as here perhaps, merely as the Buddhist name for India.

[6] This king was perhaps Kanishka himself, Fa-hien mixing up, in an inartistic way, different legends about him. Eitel suggests that a relic of the old name of the country may still exist in that of the Jats or Juts of the present day. A more common name for it is Tukhara, and he observes that the people were the Indo-Scythians of the Greeks, and the Tartars of Chinese writers, who, driven on by the Huns (180 B.C.), conquered Transoxiana, destroyed the Bactrian kingdom (126 B.C.), and finally conquered the Punjab, Cashmere, and great part of India, their greatest king being Kanishak (E. H., p. 152).

[7] Watters, clearly understanding the thought of the author in this sentence, renders--"his destiny did not extend to a connexion with the bowl;" but the term "destiny" suggests a controlling or directing power without. The king thought that his virtue in the past was not yet sufficient to give him possession of the bowl.

[8] The text is simply "those in white clothes." This may mean "the laity," or the "upasakas;" but it is better to take the characters in their common Chinese acceptation, as meaning "commoners," "men who have no rank." See in Williams' Dictionary under {.}.

[9] I do not wonder that Remusat should give for this--"et s'en retournent apres." But Fa-hien's use of {.} in the sense of "in the same way" is uniform throughout the narrative.

[10] Hardy's M. B., p. 183, says:--"The alms-bowl, given by Mahabrahma, having vanished (about the time that Gotama became Buddha), each of the four guardian deities brought him an alms-bowl of emerald, but he did not accept them. They then brought four bowls made of stone, of the colour of the mung fruit; and when each entreated that his own bowl might be accepted, Buddha caused them to appear as if formed into a single bowl, appearing at the upper rim as if placed one within the other." See the account more correctly given in the "Buddhist Birth Stories," p. 110.

[11] Compare the narrative in Luke's Gospel, xxi. 1-4.

[12] See chapter viii.

[13] This, no doubt, should be Hwuy-ying. King was at this time ill in Nagara, and indeed afterwards he dies in crossing the Little Snowy Mountains; but all the texts make him die twice. The confounding of the two names has been pointed out by Chinese critics.

[14] "Came to his end;" i.e., according to the text, "proved the impermanence and uncertainty," namely, of human life. See Williams' Dictionary under {.}. The phraseology is wholly Buddhistic.

CHAPTER XIII

NAGARA. FESTIVAL OF BUDDHA'S SKULL-BONE. OTHER RELICS, AND HIS SHADOW.

Going west for sixteen yojanas,[1] he came to the city He-lo[2] in the borders of the country of Nagara, where there is the flat-bone of Buddha's skull, deposited in a vihara[3] adorned all over with gold- leaf and the seven sacred substances. The king of the country, revering and honouring the bone, and anxious lest it should be stolen away, has selected eight individuals, representing the great families in the kingdom, and committing to each a seal, with which he should seal (its shrine) and guard (the relic). At early dawn these eight men come, and after each has inspected his seal, they open the door. This done, they wash their hands with scented water and bring out the bone, which they place outside the vihara, on a lofty platform, where it is supported on a round pedestal of the seven precious substances, and covered with a bell of /lapis lazuli/, both adorned with rows of pearls. Its colour is of a yellowish white, and it forms an imperfect circle twelve inches round,[4] curving upwards to the centre. Every day, after it has been brought forth, the keepers of the vihara ascend a high gallery, where they beat great drums, blow conchs, and clash their copper cymbals. When the king hears them, he goes to the vihara, and makes his offerings of flowers and incense. When he has done this, he (and his attendants) in order, one after another, (raise the bone), place it (for a moment) on the top of their heads,[5] and then depart, going out by the door on the west as they entered by that on the east. The king every morning makes his offerings and performs his worship, and afterwards gives audience on the business of his government. The chiefs of the Vaisyas[6] also make their offerings before they attend to their family affairs. Every day it is so, and there is no remissness in the observance of the custom. When all the offerings are over, they replace the bone in the vihara, where there is a vimoksha tope,[7] of the seven precious substances, and rather more than five cubits high, sometimes open, sometimes shut, to contain it. In front of the door of the vihara, there are parties who every morning sell flowers and incense,[8] and those who wish to make offerings buy some of all kinds. The kings of various countries are also constantly sending messengers with offerings. The vihara stands in a square of thirty paces, and though heaven should shake and earth be rent, this place would not move.

Going on, north from this, for a yojana, (Fa-hien) arrived at the capital of

Nagara, the place where the Bodhisattva once purchased with money five stalks of flowers, as an offering to the Dipankara Buddha.[9] In the midst of the city there is also the tope of Buddha's tooth, where offerings are made in the same way as to the flat-bone of his skull.

A yojana to the north-east of the city brought him to the mouth of a valley, where there is Buddha's pewter staff;[10] and a vihara also has been built at which offerings aremade. The staff is made of Gosirsha Chandana, and is quite sixteen or seventeen cubits long. It is contained in a wooden tube, and though a hundred or a thousand men ere to (try to) lift it, they could not move it.

Entering the mouth of the valley, and going west, he found Buddha's Sanghali,[11] where also there is reared a vihara, and offerings are made. It is a custom of the country when there is a great drought, for the people to collect in crowds, bring out the robe, pay worship to it, and make offerings, on which there is immediately a great rain from the sky.

South of the city, half a yojana, there is a rock-cavern, in a great hill fronting the south-west; and here it was that Buddha left his shadow. Looking at it from a distance of more than ten paces, you seem to see Buddha's real form, with his complexion of gold, and his characteristic marks[12] in their nicety clearly and brightly displayed. The nearer you approach, however, the fainter it becomes, as if it were only in your fancy. When the kings from the regions all around have sent skilful artists to take a copy, none of them have been able to do so. Among the people of the country there is a saying current that "the thousand Buddhas[13] must all leave their shadows here."

Rather more than four hundred paces west from the shadow, when Buddha was at the spot, he shaved his hair and clipt his nails, and proceeded, along with his disciples, to build a tope seventy or eighty cubits high, to be a model for all future topes; and it is still existing. By the side of it there is a monastery, with more than seven hundred monks in it. At this place there are as many as a thousand topes[14] of Arhans and Pratyeka Buddhas.[15]

NOTES

[1] Now in India, Fa-hien used the Indian measure of distance; but it is not possible to determine exactly what its length then was. The estimates of it are very different, and vary from four and a half or five miles to seven, and sometimes more. See the subject exhaustively treated in Davids' "Ceylon Coins and Measures," pp. 15-17.

[2] The present Hilda, west of Peshawur, and five miles south of Jellalabad.

[3] "The vihara," says Hardy, "is the residence of a recluse or priest;" and so Davids:--'the clean little hut where the mendicant lives." Our author, however, does not use the Indian name here, but the Chinese characters which express its meaning--tsing shay, "a pure dwelling." He uses the term occasionally, and evidently, in this sense; more frequently it occurs in his narrative in connexion with the Buddhist relic worship; and at first I translated it by "shrine" and "shrine-house;" but I came to the conclusion, at last, to employ always the Indian name. The first time I saw a shrine-house was, I think, in a monastery near Foo-chow;--a small pyramidical structure, about ten feet high, glittering as if with the precious substances, but all, it seemed to me, of tinsel. It was in a large apartment of the building, having many images in it. The monks said it was the most precious thing in their possession, and that if they opened it, as I begged them to do, there would be a convulsion that would destroy the whole establishment. See E. H., p. 166. The name of the province of Behar was given to it in consequence of its many viharas.

[4] According to the characters, "square, round, four inches." Hsuan-chwang says it was twelve inches round.

[5] In Williams' Dictionary, under {.}, the characters, used here, are employed in the phrase for "to degrade an officer," that is, "to remove the token of his rank worn on the crown of his head;" but to place a thing on the crown is a Buddhistic form of religious homage.

[6] The Vaisyas, or bourgeois caste of Hindu society, are described here as

49

"resident scholars."

[7] See Eitel's Handbook under the name vimoksha, which is explained as "the act of self-liberation," and "the dwelling or state of liberty." There are eight acts of liberating one's self from all subjective and objective trammels, and as many states of liberty (vimukti) resulting therefrom. They are eight degrees of self- inanition, and apparently eight stages on the way to nirvana. The tope in the text would be emblematic in some way of the general idea of the mental progress conducting to the Buddhistic consummation of existence.

[8] This incense would be in long "sticks," small and large, such as are sold to-day throughout China, as you enter the temples.

[9] "The illuminating Buddha," the twenty-fourth predecessor of Sakyamuni, and who, so long before, gave him the assurance that he would by-and-by be Buddha. See Jataka Tales, p. 23.

[10] The staff was, as immediately appears, of Gosirsha Chandana, or "sandal-wood from the Cow's-head mountain," a species of copper-brown sandal-wood, said to be produced most abundantly on a mountain of (the fabulous continent) Ullarakuru, north of mount Meru, which resembles in shape the head of a cow (E. H., pp. 42, 43). It is called a "pewter staff" from having on it a head and rings and pewter. See Watters, "China Review," viii, pp. 227, 228, and Williams' Dictionary, under {.}.

[11] Or Sanghati, the double or composite robe, part of a monk's attire, reaching from the shoulders to the knees, and fastened round the waist (E. H., p. 118).

[12] These were the "marks and beauties" on the person of a supreme Buddha. The rishi Kala Devala saw them on the body of the infant Sakya prince to the number of 328, those on the teeth, which had not yet come out, being visible to his spirit-like eyes (M. B., pp. 148, 149).

[13] Probably="all Buddhas."

[14] The number may appear too great. But see what is said on the size of topes in chapter iii, note 4.

[15] In Singhalese, Pase Buddhas; called also Nidana Buddhas, and Pratyeka Jinas, and explained by "individually intelligent," "completely intelligent," "intelligent as regards the nidanas." This, says Eitel (pp. 96, 97), is "a degree of saintship unknown to primitive Buddhism, denoting automats in ascetic life who attain to Buddhaship 'individually,' that is, without a teacher, and without being able to save others. As the ideal hermit, the Pratyeka Buddha is compared with the rhinoceros khadga that lives lonely in the wilderness. He is also called Nidana Buddha, as having mastered the twelve nidanas (the twelve links in the everlasting chain of cause and effect in the whole range of existence, the understanding of which solves the riddle of life, revealing the inanity of all forms of existence, and preparing the mind for nirvana). He is also compared to a horse, which, crossing a river, almost buries its body under the water, without, however, touching the bottom of the river. Thus in crossing samsara he 'suppresses the errors of life and thought, and the effects of habit and passion, without attaining to absolute perfection.'" Whether these Buddhas were unknown, as Eitel says, to primitive Buddhism, may be doubted. See Davids' Hibbert Lectures, p. 146.

CHAPTER XIV

DEATH OF HWUY-KING IN THE LITTLE SNOWY MOUNTAINS. LO-E. POHNA. CROSSING THE INDUS TO THE EAST.

Having stayed there till the third month of winter, Fa-hien and the two others,[1] proceeding southwards, crossed the Little Snowy mountains.[2] On them the snow lies accumulated both winter and summer. On the north (side) of the mountains, in the shade, they suddenly encountered a cold wind which made them shiver and become unable to speak. Hwuy-king could not go any farther. A white froth came from his mouth, and he said to Fa-hien, "I cannot live any longer. Do you immediately go away, that we do not all die here;" and with these words he died.[3] Fa-hien stroked the corpse, and cried out piteously, "Our original plan has failed;--it is fate.[4] What can we do?" He then again exerted himself, and they succeeded in crossing to the south of the range, and arrived in the kingdom of Lo-e,[5] where there were nearly three thousand monks, students of both the mahayana and hinayana. Here they stayed for the summer retreat,[6] and when that was over, they went on to the south, and ten days' journey brought them to the kingdom of Poh-na,[7] where there are also more than three thousand monks, all students of the hinayana. Proceeding from this place for three days, they again crossed the Indus, where the country on each side was low and level.[8]

NOTES

[1] These must have been Tao-ching and Hwuy-king.

[2] Probably the Safeid Koh, and on the way to the Kohat pass.

[3] All the texts have Kwuy-king. See chapter xii, note 13.

[4] A very natural exclamation, but out of place and inconsistent from the lips of Fa-hien. The Chinese character {.}, which he employed, may be rendered rightly by "fate" or "destiny;" but the fate is not unintelligent. The term implies a factor, or fa-tor, and supposes the ordination of Heaven or God. A Confucian idea for the moment overcame his Buddhism.

[5] Lo-e, or Rohi, is a name for Afghanistan; but only a portion of it can be here intended.

[6] We are now therefore in 404.

[7] No doubt the present district of Bannu, in the Lieutenant- Governorship of the Punjab, between 32d 10s and 33d 15s N. lat., and 70d 26s and 72d E. lon. See Hunter's Gazetteer of India, i, p. 393.

[8] They had then crossed the Indus before. They had done so, indeed, twice; first, from north to south, at Skardo or east of it; and second, as described in chapter vii.

CHAPTER XV

BHIDA. SYMPATHY OF MONKS WITH THE PILGRIMS.

After they had crossed the river, there was a country named Pe- t'oo,[1] where Buddhism was very flourishing, and (the monks) studied both the mahayana and hinayana. When they saw their fellow-disciples from Ts'in passing along, they were moved with great pity and sympathy, and expressed themselves thus: "How is it that these men from a border-land should have learned to become monks,[2] and come for the sake of our doctrines from such a distance in search of the Law of Buddha?" They supplied them with what they needed, and treated them in accordance with the rules of the Law.

NOTES

[1] Bhida. Eitel says, "The present Punjab;" i.e. it was a portion of that.

[2] "To come forth from their families;" that is, to become celibates, and adopt the tonsure.

CHAPTER XVI

ON TO MATHURA OR MUTTRA. CONDITION AND CUSTOMS OF CENTRAL INDIA; OF THE MONKS, VIHARAS, AND MONASTERIES.

From this place they travelled south-east, passing by a succession of very many monasteries, with a multitude of monks, who might be counted by myriads. After passing all these places, they came to a country named Ma-t'aou-lo.[1] They still followed the course of the P'oo-na[2] river, on the banks of which, left and right, there were twenty monasteries, which might contain three thousand monks; and (here) the Law of Buddha was still more flourishing. Everywhere, from the Sandy Desert, in all the countries of India, the kings had been firm believers in that Law. When they make their offerings to a community of monks, they take off their royal caps, and along with their relatives and ministers, supply them with food with their own hands. That done, (the king) has a carpet spread for himself on the ground, and sits down in front of the chairman;--they dare not presume to sit on couches in front of the community. The laws and ways, according to which the kings presented their offerings when Buddha was in the world, have been handed down to the present day.

All south from this is named the Middle Kingdom.[3] In it the cold and heat are finely tempered, and there is neither hoarfrost nor snow. The people are numerous and happy; they have not to register their households, or attend to any magistrates and their rules; only those who cultivate the royal land have to pay (a portion of) the grain from it. If they want to go, they go; if they want to stay on, they stay. The king governs without decapitation or (other) corporal punishments. Criminals are simply fined, lightly or heavily, according to the circumstances (of each case). Even in cases of repeated attempts at wicked rebellion, they only have their right hands cut off. The king's body-guards and attendants all have salaries. Throughout the whole country the people do not kill any living creature, nor drink intoxicating liquor, nor eat onions or garlic. The only exception is that of the Chandalas.[4] That is the name for those who are (held to be) wicked men, and live apart from others. When they enter the gate of a city or a market-place, they strike a piece of wood to make themselves known, so that men know and avoid them, and do not come into contact with them. In that country they do not keep pigs and fowls, and do not sell live cattle; in the markets there are no butchers' shops and no dealers in intoxicating drink. In buying and selling commodities they use cowries.[5] Only the Chandalas are fishermen and hunters, and sell flesh meat.

After Buddha attained to pari-nirvana,[6] the kings of the various countries and the heads of the Vaisyas[7] built viharas for the priests, and endowed them with fields, houses, gardens, and orchards, along with the resident populations and their cattle, the grants being engraved on plates of metal,[8] so that afterwards they were handed down from king to king, without any daring to annul them, and they remain even to the present time.

The regular business of the monks is to perform acts of meritorious virtue, and to recite their Sutras and sit wrapt in meditation. When stranger monks arrive (at any monastery), the old residents meet and receive them, carry for them their clothes and alms-bowl, give them water to wash their feet, oil with which to anoint them, and the liquid food permitted out of the regular hours.[9] When (the stranger) has enjoyed a very brief rest, they further ask the number of years that he has been a monk, after which he receives a sleeping apartment with its appurtenances, according to his regular order, and everything is done for him which the rules prescribe.[10]

Where a community of monks resides, they erect topes to Sariputtra,[11] to Maha-maudgalyayana,[12] and to Ananda,[13] and also topes (in honour) of the Abhidharma, the Vinaya, and the Sutras. A month after the (annual season of) rest, the families which are looking out for blessing stimulate one another[14] to make offerings to the monks, and send round to them the liquid food which may be taken out of the ordinary hours. All the monks come together in a great assembly, and preach the Law;[15] after which offerings are presented at the tope of Sariputtra, with all kinds of flowers and incense. All through the night lamps are kept burning, and skilful musicians are employed to perform.[16]

When Sariputtra was a great Brahman, he went to Buddha, and begged (to be permitted) to quit his family (and become a monk). The great Mugalan and the great Kasyapa[17] also did the same. The bhikshunis[18] for the most part make their offerings at the tope of Ananda, because it was he who requested the World-honoured one to allow females to quit their families (and become nuns). The Sramaneras[19] mostly make their offerings to Rahula.[20] The professors of the Abhidharma make their offerings to it; those of the Vinaya to it. Every year there is one such offering, and each class has its own day for it. Students of the mahayana present offerings to the Prajna-paramita,[21] to Manjusri,[22] and to Kwan-she-yin.[23] When the monks have done receiving their annual tribute (from the harvests),[24] the Heads of the Vaisyas and all the Brahmans bring clothes and other such articles as the monks require for use, and distribute among them. The monks, having received them, also proceed to give portions to one another. From the nirvana of Buddha,[25] the forms of ceremony, laws, and rules, practised by the sacred communities, have been handed down from one generation to another without interruption.

From the place where (the travellers) crossed the Indus to Southern India, and on to the Southern Sea, a distance of forty or fifty thousand le, all is level plain. There are no large hills with streams (among them); there are simply the waters of the rivers.

NOTES

[1] Muttra, "the peacock city;" lat. 27d 30s N., lon. 77d 43s E. (Hunter); the birthplace of Krishna, whose emblem is the peacock.

[2] This must be the Jumna, or Yamuna. Why it is called, as here, the P'oo-na has yet to be explained.

[3] In Pali, Majjhima-desa, "the Middle Country." See Davids' "Buddhist Birth Stories," page 61, note.

[4] Eitel (pp. 145, 6) says, "The name Chandalas is explained by 'butchers,' 'wicked men,' and those who carry 'the awful flag,' to warn off their betters;--the lowest and most despised caste of India, members of which, however, when converted, were admitted even into the ranks of the priesthood."

[5] "Cowries;" {.} {.}, not "shells and ivory," as one might suppose; but cowries alone, the second term entering into the name from the marks inside the edge of the shell, resembling "the teeth of fishes."

[6] See chapter xii, note 3, Buddha's pari-nirvana is equivalent to Buddha's death.

[7] See chapter xiii, note 6. The order of the characters is different here, but with the same meaning.

[8] See the preparation of such a deed of grant in a special case, as related in chapter xxxix. No doubt in Fa-hien's time, and long before and after it, it was the custom to engrave such deeds on plates of metal.

[9] "No monk can eat solid food except between sunrise and noon," and total abstinence from intoxicating drinks is obligatory (Davids' Manual, p. 163). Food eaten at any other part of the day is called vikala, and forbidden; but a weary traveller might receive unseasonable refreshment, consisting, as Watters has shown (Ch. Rev. viii. 282), of honey, butter, treacle, and sesamum oil.

[10] The expression here is somewhat perplexing; but it occurs again in chapter xxxviii; and the meaning is clear. See Watters, Ch. Rev. viii. 282, 3. The rules are given at length in the Sacred Books of the East, vol. xx, p. 272 and foll., and p. 279 and foll.

[11] Sariputtra (Singh. Seriyut) was one of the principal disciples of Buddha, and indeed the most learned and ingenious of them all, so that he obtained the title of {.} {.}, "knowledge and wisdom." He is also called Buddha's "right-hand attendant." His name is derived from that of his mother Sarika, the wife of Tishya, a native of Nalanda. In Spence Hardy, he often appears under the name of Upatissa (Upa- tishya), derived from his father. Several Sastras are ascribed to him, and indeed the followers of the Abhidharma look on him as their founder. He died before Sakyamuni; but is to reappear as a future Buddha. Eitel, pp. 123, 124.

[12] Mugalan, the Singhalese name of this disciple, is more pronounceable. He also was one of the principal disciples, called Buddha's "left-hand attendant." He was distinguished for his power of vision, and his magical powers. The name in the text is derived from the former attribute, and it was by the latter that he took up an artist to Tushita to get a view of Sakyamuni, and so make a statue of him. (Compare the similar story in chap. vi.) He went to hell, and released his mother. He also died before Sakyamuni, and is to reappear as Buddha. Eitel, p. 65.

[13] See chapter xii, note 2.

[14] A passage rather difficult to construe. The "families" would be those more devout than their neighbours.

[15] One rarely hears this preaching in China. It struck me most as I once heard it at Osaka in Japan. There was a pulpit in a large hall of the temple, and the audience sat around on the matted floor. One priest took the pulpit after another; and the hearers nodded their heads occasionally, and indicated their sympathy now and then by an audible "h'm," which reminded me of Carlyle's description of meetings of "The Ironsides" of Cromwell.

[16] This last statement is wanting in the Chinese editions.

[17] There was a Kasyapa Buddha, anterior to Sakyamuni. But this Maha-kasyapa was a Brahman of Magadha, who was converted by Buddha, and became one of his disciples. He took the lead after Sakyamuni's death, convoked and directed the first synod, from which his title of Arya- sthavira is derived. As the first compiler of the Canon, he is considered the fountain of Chinese orthodoxy, and counted as the first patriarch. He also is to be reborn as Buddha. Eitel, p. 64.

[18] The bhikshunis are the female monks or nuns, subject to the same rules as the bhikshus, and also to special ordinances of restraint. See Hardy's E. M., chap. 17. See also Sacred Books of the East, vol. xx, p. 321.

[19] The Sramaneras are the novices, male or female, who have vowed to observe the Shikshapada, or ten commandments. Fa-hien was himself one of them from his childhood. Having heard the Trisharana, or threefold formula of Refuge,--"I take refuge in Buddha; the Law; the Church,-- the novice undertakes to observe the ten precepts that forbid --(1) destroying life; (2) stealing; (3) impurity; (4) lying; (5) intoxicating drinks; (6) eating after midday; (7) dancing, singing, music, and stage-plays; (8) garlands, scents, unguents, and ornaments; (9) high or broad couches; (10) receiving gold or silver." Davids' Manual, p. 160; Hardy's E. M., pp. 23, 24.

[20] The eldest son of Sakyamuni by Yasodhara. Converted to Buddhism, he followed his father as an attendant; and after Buddha's death became the founder of a philosophical realistic school (vaibhashika). He is now revered as the patron saint of all novices, and is to be reborn as the eldest son of

every future Buddha. Eitel, p. 101. His mother also is to be reborn as Buddha.

[21] There are six (sometimes increased to ten) paramitas, "means of passing to nirvana:--Charity; morality; patience; energy; tranquil contemplation; wisdom (prajna); made up to ten by use of the proper means; science; pious vows; and force of purpose. But it is only prajna which carries men across the samsara to the shores of nirvana." Eitel, p. 90.

[22] According to Eitel (pp. 71, 72), "A famous Bodhisattva, now specially worshipped in Shan-se, whose antecedents are a hopeless jumble of history and fable. Fa-hien found him here worshipped by followers of the mahayana school; but Hsuan-chwang connects his worship with the yogachara or tantra-magic school. The mahayana school regard him as the apotheosis of perfect wisdom. His most common titles are Mahamati, "Great wisdom," and Kumara-raja, "King of teaching, with a thousand arms and a hundred alms-bowls."

[23] Kwan-she-yin and the dogmas about him or her are as great a mystery as Manjusri. The Chinese name is a mistranslation of the Sanskrit name Avalokitesvra, "On-looking Sovereign," or even "On- looking Self-Existent," and means "Regarding or Looking on the sounds of the world,"="Hearer of Prayer." Originally, and still in Thibet, Avalokitesvara had only male attributes, but in China and Japan (Kwannon), this deity (such popularly she is) is represented as a woman, "Kwan-yin, the greatly gentle, with a thousand arms and a thousand eyes;" and has her principal seat in the island of P'oo-t'oo, on the China coast, which is a regular place of pilgrimage. To the worshippers of whom Fa-hien speaks, Kwan-she-yin would only be Avalokitesvara. How he was converted into the "goddess of mercy," and her worship took the place which it now has in China, is a difficult inquiry, which would take much time and space, and not be brought after all, so far as I see, to a satisfactory conclusion. See Eitel's Handbook, pp. 18-20, and his Three Lectures on Buddhism (third edition), pp. 124-131. I was talking on the subject once with an intelligent Chinese gentleman, when he remarked, "Have you not much the same thing in Europe in the worship of Mary?"

[24] Compare what is said in chap. v.

[25] This nirvana of Buddha must be--not his death, but his attaining to Buddhaship.

CHAPTER XVII

SANKASYA. BUDDHA'S ASCENT TO AND DESCENT FROM THE TRAYASTRIMSAS HEAVEN, AND OTHER LEGENDS.

From this they proceeded south-east for eighteen yojanas, and found themselves in a kingdom called Sankasya,[1] at the place where Buddha came down, after ascending to the Trayastrimsas heaven,[2] and there preaching for three months his Law for the benefit of his mother.[3] Buddha had gone up to this heaven by his supernatural power,[4] without letting his disciples know; but seven days before the completion (of the three months) he laid aside his invisibility,[4] and Anuruddha,[5] with his heavenly eyes,[5] saw the World-honoured one, and immediately said to the honoured one, the great Mugalan, "Do you go and salute the World-honoured one." Mugalan forthwith went, and with head and face did homage at (Buddha's) feet. They then saluted and questioned each other, and when this was over, Buddha said to Mugalan, "Seven days after this I will go down to Jambudvipa;" and thereupon Mugalan returned. At this time the great kings of eight countries with their ministers and people, not having seen Buddha for a long time, were all thirstily looking up for him, and had collected in clouds in this kingdom to wait for the World-honoured one.

Then the bhikshuni Utpala[6] thought in her heart, "To-day the kings, with their ministers and people, will all be meeting (and welcoming) Buddha. I am (but) a woman; how shall I succeed in being the first to see him?"[7] Buddha immediately, by his spirit-like power, changed her into the appearance of a holy Chakravartti[8] king, and she was the foremost of all in doing reverence to him.

As Buddha descended from his position aloft in the Trayastrimsas heaven,

60

when he was coming down, there were made to appear three flights of precious steps. Buddha was on the middle flight, the steps of which were composed of the seven precious substances. The king of Brahma-loka[9] also made a flight of silver steps appear on the right side, (where he was seen) attending with a white chowry in his hand. Sakra, Ruler of Devas, made (a flight of) steps of purple gold on the left side, (where he was seen) attending and holding an umbrella of the seven precious substances. An innumerable multitude of the devas followed Buddha in his descent. When he was come down, the three flights all disappeared in the ground, excepting seven steps, which continued to be visible. Afterwards king Asoka, wishing to know where their ends rested, sent men to dig and see. They went down to the yellow springs[10] without reaching the bottom of the steps, and from this the king received an increase to his reverence and faith, and built a vihara over the steps, with a standing image, sixteen cubits in height, right over the middle flight. Behind the vihara he erected a stone pillar, about fifty cubits high,[11] with a lion on the top of it.[12] Let into the pillar, on each of its four sides,[13] there is an image of Buddha, inside and out[14] shining and transparent, and pure as it were of /lapis lazuli/. Some teachers of another doctrine[15] once disputed with the Sramanas about (the right to) this as a place of residence, and the latter were having the worst of the argument, when they took an oath on both sides on the condition that, if the place did indeed belong to the Sramanas, there should be some marvellous attestation of it. When these words had been spoken, the lion on the top gave a great roar, thus giving the proof; on which their opponents were frightened, bowed to the decision, and withdrew.

Through Buddha having for three months partaken of the food of heaven, his body emitted a heavenly fragrance, unlike that of an ordinary man. He went immediately and bathed; and afterwards, at the spot where he did so, a bathing-house was built, which is still existing. At the place where the bhikshuni Utpala was the first to do reverence to Buddha, a tope has now been built.

At the places where Buddha, when he was in the world, cut his hair and nails, topes are erected; and where the three Buddhas[16] that preceded Sakyamuni Buddha and he himself sat; where they walked,[17] and where images of their persons were made. At all these places topes were made, and are still existing. At the place where Sakra, Ruler of the Devas, and the king of the Brahma-loka followed Buddha down (from the Trayastrimsas heaven) they have also raised a tope.

At this place the monks and nuns may be a thousand, who all receive their food from the common store, and pursue their studies, some of the mahayana and some of the hinayana. Where they live, there is a white-eared dragon, which acts the part of danapati to the community of these monks, causing abundant harvests in the country, and the enriching rains to come in season, without the occurrence of any calamities, so that the monks enjoy their repose and ease. In gratitude for its kindness, they have made for it a dragon-house, with a carpet for it to sit on, and appointed for it a diet of blessing, which they present for its nourishment. Every day they set apart three of their number to go to its house, and eat there. Whenever the summer retreat is ended, the dragon straightway changes its form, and appears as a small snake,[18] with white spots at the side of its ears. As soon as the monks recognise it, they fill a copper vessel with cream, into which they put the creature, and then carry it round from the one who has the highest seat (at their tables) to him who has the lowest, when it appears as if saluting them. When it has been taken round, immediately it disappeared; and every year it thus comes forth once. The country is very productive, and the people are prosperous, and happy beyond comparison. When people of other countries come to it, they are exceedingly attentive to them all, and supply them with what they need.

Fifty yojanas north-west from the monastery there is another, called "The Great Heap."[19] Great Heap was the name of a wicked demon, who was converted by Buddha, and men subsequently at this place reared a vihara. When it was being made over to an Arhat by pouring water on his hands,[20] some drops fell on the ground. They are still on the spot, and however they may be brushed away and removed, they continue to be visible, and cannot be made to disappear.

At this place there is also a tope to Buddha, where a good spirit constantly keeps (all about it) swept and watered, without any labour of man being required. A king of corrupt views once said, "Since you are able to do this, I will lead a multitude of troops and reside there till the dirt and filth has increased and accumulated, and (see) whether you can cleanse it away or not." The spirit thereupon raised a great wind, which blew (the filth away), and made the place pure.

At this place there are a hundred small topes, at which a man may keep counting a whole day without being able to know (their exact number). If he be firmly bent on knowing it, he will place a man by the side of each tope. When this is done, proceeding to count the number of men, whether they be many or few, he will not get to know (the number).[21]

There is a monastery, containing perhaps 600 or 700 monks, in which there is a place where a Pratyeka Buddha used to take his food. The nirvana ground (where he was burned[22] after death) is as large as a carriage wheel; and while grass grows all around, on this spot there is none. The ground also where he dried his clothes produces no grass, but the impression of them, where they lay on it, continues to the present day.

NOTES

[1] The name is still remaining in Samkassam, a village forty-five miles northwest of Canouge, lat. 27d 3s N., lon. 79d 50s E.

[2] The heaven of Indra or Sakya, meaning "the heaven of thirty-three classes," a name which has been explained both historically and mythologically. "The description of it," says Eitel, p. 148, "tallies in all respects with the Svarga of Brahmanic mythology. It is situated between the four peaks of the Meru, and consists of thirty-two cities of devas, eight one each of the four corners of the mountain. Indra's capital of Bellevue is in the centre. There he is enthroned, with a thousand heads and a thousand eyes, and four arms grasping the vajra, with his wife and 119,000 concubines. There he receives the monthly reports of the four Maharajas, concerning the progress of good and evil in the world," &c. &c.

[3] Buddha's mother, Maya and Mahamaya, the /mater immaculata/ of the

Buddhists, died seven days after his birth. Eitel says, "Reborn in Tushita, she was visited there by her son and converted." The Tushita heaven was a more likely place to find her than the Trayastrimsas; but was the former a part of the latter? Hardy gives a long account of Buddha's visit to the Trayastrimsas (M. B., pp. 298-302), which he calls Tawutisa, and speaks of his mother (Matru) in it, who had now become a deva by the changing of her sex.

[4] Compare the account of the Arhat's conveyance of the artist to the Tushita heaven in chap. v. The first expression here is more comprehensive.

[5] Anuruddha was a first cousin of Sakyamuni, being the son of his uncle Amritodana. He is often mentioned in the account we have of Buddha's last moments. His special gift was the divyachakshus or "heavenly eye," the first of the six abhijnas or "supernatural talents," the faculty of comprehending in one instantaneous view, or by intuition, all beings in all worlds. "He could see," says Hardy, M. B., p. 232, "all things in 100,000 sakvalas as plainly as a mustard seed held in the hand."

[6] Eitel gives the name Utpala with the same Chinese phonetisation as in the text, but not as the name of any bhikshuni. The Sanskrit word, however, is explained by "blue lotus flowers;" and Hsuan-chwang calls her the nun "Lotus-flower colour ({.} {.} {.});"--the same as Hardy's Upulwan and Uppalawarna.

[7] Perhaps we should read here "to see Buddha," and then ascribe the transformation to the nun herself. It depends on the punctuation which view we adopt; and in the structure of the passage, there is nothing to indicate that the stop should be made before or after "Buddha." And the one view is as reasonable, or rather as unreasonable, as the other.

[8] "A holy king who turns the wheel;" that is, the military conqueror and monarch of the whole or part of a universe. "The symbol," says Eitel (p. 142) "of such a king is the chakra or wheel, for when he ascends the throne, a chakra falls from heaven, indicating by its material (gold, silver, copper, or iron) the extent and character of his reign. The office, however, of the highest Chakravartti, who hurls his wheel among his enemies, is inferior to

the peaceful mission of a Buddha, who meekly turns the wheel of the Law, and conquers every universe by his teaching."

[9] This was Brahma, the first person of the Brahmanical Trimurti, adopted by Buddhism, but placed in an inferior position, and surpassed by every Buddhist saint who attains to bodhi.

[10] A common name for the earth below, where, on digging, water is found.

[11] The height is given as thirty chow, the chow being the distance from the elbow to the finger-tip, which is variously estimated.

[12] A note of Mr. Beal says on this:--"General Cunningham, who visited the spot (1862), found a pillar, evidently of the age of Asoka, with a well-carved elephant on the top, which, however, was minus trunk and tail. He supposes this to be the pillar seen by Fa-hien, who mistook the top of it for a lion. It is possible such a mistake may have been made, as in the account of one of the pillars at Sravasti, Fa-hien says an ox formed the capital, whilst Hsuan-chwang calls it an elephant (P. 19, Arch. Survey)."

[13] That is, in niches on the sides. The pillar or column must have been square.

[14] Equivalent to "all through."

[15] Has always been translated "heretical teachers;" but I eschew the terms /heresy/ and /heretical/. The parties would not be Buddhists of any creed or school, but Brahmans or of some other false doctrine, as Fa-hien deemed it. The Chinese term means "outside" or "foreign;"--in Pali, anna-titthiya,="those belonging to another school."

[16] These three predecessors of Sakyamuni were the three Buddhas of the present or Maha-bhadra Kalpa, of which he was the fourth, and Maitreya is to be the fifth and last. They were: (1) Krakuchanda (Pali, Kakusanda), "he who readily solves all doubts;" a scion of the Kasyapa family. Human life

reached in his time 40,000 years, and so many persons were converted by him. (2) Kanakamuni (Pali, Konagamana), "body radiant with the colour of pure gold;" of the same family. Human life reached in his time 30,000 years, and so many persons were converted by him. (3) Kasyapa (Pali, Kassapa), "swallower of light." Human life reached in his time 20,000 years, and so many persons were converted by him. See Eitel, under the several names; Hardy's M. B., pp. 95-97; and Davids' "Buddhist Birth Stories," p. 51.

[17] That is, walked in meditation. Such places are called Chankramana (Pali, Chankama); promenades or corridors connected with a monastery, made sometimes with costly stones, for the purpose of peripatetic meditation. The "sitting" would be not because of weariness or for rest, but for meditation. E. H., p. 144.

[18] The character in my Corean copy is {.}, which must be a mistake for the {.} of the Chinese editions. Otherwise, the meaning would be "a small medusa."

[19] The reading here seems to me a great improvement on that of the Chinese editions, which means "Fire Limit." Buddha, it is said, {.} converted this demon, which Chinese character Beal rendered at first by "in one of his incarnations;" and in his revised version he has "himself." The difference between Fa-hien's usage of {.} and {.} throughout his narrative is quite marked. {.} always refers to the doings of Sakyamuni; {.}, "formerly," is often used of him and others in the sense of "in a former age or birth."

[20] See Hardy, M. B., p. 194:--"As a token of the giving over of the garden, the king poured water upon the hands of Buddha; and from this time it became one of the principal residences of the sage."

[21] This would seem to be absurd; but the writer evidently intended to convey the idea that there was something mysterious about the number of the topes.

[22] This seems to be the meaning. The bodies of the monks are all burned. Hardy's E. M., pp. 322-324.

CHAPTER XVIII

KANYAKUBJA, OR CANOUGE. BUDDHA'S PREACHING.

Fa-hien stayed at the Dragon vihara till after the summer retreat,[1] and then, travelling to the south-east for seven yojanas, he arrived at the city of Kanyakubja,[2] lying along the Ganges.[3] There are two monasteries in it, the inmates of which are students of the hinayana. At a distance from the city of six or seven le, on the west, on the northern bank of the Ganges, is a place where Buddha preached the Law to his disciples. It has been handed down that his subjects of discourse were such as "The bitterness and vanity (of life) as impermanent and uncertain," and that "The body is as a bubble or foam on the water." At this spot a tope was erected, and still exists.

Having crossed the Ganges, and gone south for three yojanas, (the travellers) arrived at a village named A-le,[4] containing places where Buddha preached the Law, where he sat, and where he walked, at all of which topes have been built.

NOTES

[1] We are now, probably, in 405.

[2] Canouge, the latitude and longitude of which have been given in a previous note. The Sanskrit name means "the city of humpbacked maidens;" with reference to the legend of the hundred daughters of king Brahma-datta, who were made deformed by the curse of the rishi Maha-vriksha, whose overtures they had refused. E. H., p. 51.

[3] Ganga, explained by "Blessed water," and "Come from heaven to earth."

[4] This village (the Chinese editions read "forest") has hardly been clearly identified.

CHAPTER XIX

SHA-CHE. LEGEND OF BUDDHA'S DANTA-KASHTHA.

Going on from this to the south-east for three yojanas, they came to the great kingdom of Sha-che.[1] As you go out of the city of Sha-che by the southern gate, on the east of the road (is the place) where Buddha, after he had chewed his willow branch,[2] stuck it in the ground, when it forthwith grew up seven cubits, (at which height it remained) neither increasing nor diminishing. The Brahmans with their contrary doctrines[3] became angry and jealous. Sometimes they cut the tree down, sometimes they plucked it up, and cast it to a distance, but it grew again on the same spot as at first. Here also is the place where the four Buddhas walked and sat, and at which a tope was built that is still existing.

NOTES

[1] Sha-che should probably be Sha-khe, making Cunningham's identification of the he present Saket still more likely. The change of {.} into {.} is slight; and, indeed, the Khang-hsi dictionary thinks the two characters should be but one and the same.

[2] This was, no doubt, what was called the danta-kashtha, or "dental wood," mostly a bit of the /ficus Indicus/ or banyan tree, which the monk chews every morning to cleanse his teeth, and for the purpose of health generally. The Chinese, not having the banyan, have used, or at least Fa-hien used, Yang ({.}, the general name for the willow) instead of it.

[3] Are two classes of opponents, or only one, intended here, so that we should read "all the unbelievers and Brahmans," or "heretics and Brahmans?" I think the Brahmans were also "the unbelievers" and "heretics," having {.} {.}, views and ways outside of, and opposed to, Buddha's.

CHAPTER XX

KOSALA AND SRAVASTI. THE JETAVANA VIHARA AND OTHER MEMORIALS AND LEGENDS OF BUDDHA. SYMPATHY OF THE MONKS WITH THE PILGRIMS.

Going on from this to the south, for eight yojanas, (the travellers) came to the city of Sravasti[1] in the kingdom of Kosala,[2] in which the inhabitants were few and far between, amounting in all (only) to a few more than two hundred families; the city where king Prasenajit[3] ruled, and the place of the old vihara of Maha-prajapti;[4] of the well and walls of (the house of) the (Vaisya) head Sudatta;[5] and where the Angulimalya[6] became an Arhat, and his body was (afterwards) burned on his attaining to pari-nirvana. At all these places topes were subsequently erected, which are still existing in the city. The Brahmans, with their contrary doctrine, became full of hatred and envy in their hearts, and wished to destroy them, but there came from the heavens such a storm of crashing thunder and flashing lightning that they were not able in the end to effect their purpose.

As you go out from the city by the south gate, and 1,200 paces from it, the (Vaisya) head Sudatta built a vihara, facing the south; and when the door was open, on each side of it there was a stone pillar, with the figure of a wheel on the top of that on the left, and the figure of an ox on the top of that on the right. On the left and right of the building the ponds of water clear and pure, the thickets of trees always luxuriant, and the numerous flowers of various hues, constituted a lovely scene, the whole forming what is called the Jetavana vihara.[7]

When Buddha went up to the Trayastrimsas heaven,[8] and preached the Law for the benefit of his mother, (after he had been absent for) ninety days, Prasenajit, longing to see him, caused an image of him to be carved in Gosirsha Chandana wood,[9] and put in the place where he usually sat. When Buddha on his return entered the vihara, Buddha said to it, "Return to your seat. After I have attained to pari-nirvana, you will serve as a pattern to the four classes of my disciples,"[10] and on this the image returned to its seat. This was the very first of all the images (of Buddha), and that which men subsequently copied. Buddha then removed, and dwelt in a small vihara on the south side (of the other), a different place from that containing the image, and twenty paces distant from it.

The Jetavana vihara was originally of seven storeys. The kings and people of the countries around vied with one another in their offerings, hanging up about it silken streamers and canopies, scattering flowers, burning incense, and lighting lamps, so as to make the night as bright as the day. This they did day after day without ceasing. (It happened that) a rat, carrying in its mouth the wick of a lamp, set one of the streamers or canopies on fire, which caught the vihara, and the seven storeys were all consumed. The kings, with their officers and people, were all very sad and distressed, supposing that the sandal-wood image had been burned; but lo! after four or five days, when the door of a small vihara on the east was opened, there was immediately seen the original image. They were all greatly rejoiced, and co-operated in restoring the vihara. When they had succeeded in completing two storeys, they removed the image back to its former place.

When Fa-hien and Tao-ching first arrived at the Jetavana monastery, and thought how the World-honoured one had formerly resided there for twenty-five years, painful reflections arose in their minds. Born in a border-land, along with their like-minded friends, they had travelled through so many kingdoms; some of those friends had returned (to their own land), and some had (died), proving the impermanence and uncertainty of life; and to-day they saw the place where Buddha had lived now unoccupied by him. They were melancholy through their pain of heart, and the crowd of monks came out, and asked them from what kingdom they were come. "We are come," they replied, "from the land of Han." "Strange," said the monks with a sigh, "that men of a border country should be able to come here in search of our Law!" Then they said to one another, "During all the time that we, preceptors and monks,[11] have succeeded to one another, we have never seen men of Han, followers of our system, arrive here."

Four le to the north-west of the vihara there is a grove called "The Getting of Eyes." Formerly there were five hundred blind men, who lived here in order that they might be near the vihara.[12] Buddha preached his Law to them, and they all got back their eyesight. Full of joy, they stuck their staves in the earth, and with their heads and faces on the ground, did reverence. The staves immediately began to grow, and they grew to be great. People made much of them, and no one dared to cut them down, so that they came to form a grove. It was in this way that it got its name, and most of the Jetavana monks, after they had taken their midday meal, went to the grove, and sat there in meditation.

Six or seven le north-east from the Jetavana, mother Vaisakha[13] built another vihara, to which she invited Buddha and his monks, and which is still existing.

To each of the great residences for monks at the Jetavana vihara there were two gates, one facing the east and the other facing the north. The park (containing the whole) was the space of ground which the (Vaisya) head Sudatta purchased by covering it with gold coins. The vihara was exactly in the centre. Here Buddha lived for a longer time than at any other place, preaching his Law and converting men. At the places where he walked and sat they also (subsequently) reared topes, each having its particular name; and here was the place where Sundari[14] murdered a person and then falsely charged Buddha (with the crime). Outside the east gate of the Jetavana, at a distance of seventy paces to the north, on the west of the road, Buddha held a discussion with the (advocates of the) ninety-six schemes of erroneous doctrine, when the king and his great officers, the householders, and people were all assembled in crowds to hear it. Then a woman belonging to one of the erroneous systems, by name Chanchamana,[15] prompted by the envious hatred in her heart, and having put on (extra) clothes in front of her person, so as to give her the appearance of being with child, falsely accused Buddha before all the assembly of having acted unlawfully (towards her). On this, Sakra, Ruler of Devas, changed himself and some devas into white mice, which bit through the strings about her waist; and when this was done, the (extra) clothes which she wore dropt down on the ground. The earth at the same time was rent, and she went (down) alive into hell.[16] (This) also is the place where Devadatta,[17] trying with empoisoned claws to injure Buddha, went down alive into hell. Men subsequently set up marks to distinguish where both these events took place.

Further, at the place where the discussion took place, they reared a vihara
71

rather more than sixty cubits high, having in it an image of Buddha in a sitting posture. On the east of the road there was a devalaya[18] of (one of) the contrary systems, called "The Shadow Covered," right opposite the vihara on the place of discussion, with (only) the road between them, and also rather more than sixty cubits high. The reason why it was called "The Shadow Covered" was this:-- When the sun was in the west, the shadow of the vihara of the World- honoured one fell on the devalaya of a contrary system; but when the sun was in the east, the shadow of that devalaya was diverted to the north, and never fell on the vihara of Buddha. The mal-believers regularly employed men to watch their devalaya, to sweep and water (all about it), to burn incense, light the lamps, and present offerings; but in the morning the lamps were found to have been suddenly removed, and in the vihara of Buddha. The Brahmans were indignant, and said, "Those Sramanas take out lamps and use them for their own service of Buddha, but we will not stop our service for you!"[19] On that night the Brahmans themselves kept watch, when they saw the deva spirits which they served take the lamps and go three times round the vihara of Buddha and present offerings. After this ministration to Buddha they suddenly disappeared. The Brahmans thereupon knowing how great was the spiritual power of Buddha, forthwith left their families, and became monks.[20] It has been handed down, that, near the time when these things occurred, around the Jetavana vihara there were ninety-eight monasteries, in all of which there were monks residing, excepting only in one place which was vacant. In this Middle Kingdom[21] there are ninety-six[21] sorts of views, erroneous and different from our system, all of which recognise this world and the future world[22] (and the connexion between them). Each had its multitude of followers, and they all beg their food: only they do not carry the alms-bowl. They also, moreover, seek (to acquire) the blessing (of good deeds) on unfrequented ways, setting up on the road-side houses of charity, where rooms, couches, beds, and food and drink are supplied to travellers, and also to monks, coming and going as guests, the only difference being in the time (for which those parties remain).

There are also companies of the followers of Devadatta still existing. They regularly make offerings to the three previous Buddhas, but not to Sakyamuni Buddha.

Four le south-east from the city of Sravasti, a tope has been erected at the place where the World-honoured one encountered king Virudhaha,[23] when he wished to attack the kingdom of Shay-e,[23] and took his stand before him at the side of the road.[24]

NOTES

[1] In Singhalese, Sewet; here evidently the capital of Kosala. It is placed by Cunningham (Archaeological Survey) on the south bank of the Rapti, about fifty-eight miles north of Ayodya or Oude. There are still the ruins of a great town, the name being Sahet Mahat. It was in this town, or in its neighbourhood, that Sakyamuni spent many years of his life after he became Buddha.

[2] There were two Indian kingdoms of this name, a southern and a northern. This was the northern, a part of the present Oudh.

[3] In Singhalese, Pase-nadi, meaning "leader of the victorious army." He was one of the earliest converts and chief patrons of Sakyamuni. Eitel calls him (p. 95) one of the originators of Buddhist idolatory, because of the statue which is mentioned in this chapter. See Hardy's M. B., pp. 283, 284, et al.

[4] Explained by "Path of Love," and "Lord of Life." Prajapati was aunt and nurse of Sakyamuni, the first woman admitted to the monkhood, and the first superior of the first Buddhistic convent. She is yet to become a Buddha.

[5] Sudatta, meaning "almsgiver," was the original name of Anatha-pindika (or Pindada), a wealthy householder, or Vaisya head, of Sravasti, famous for his liberality (Hardy, Anepidu). Of his old house, only the well and walls remained at the time of Fa-hien's visit to Sravasti.

[6] The Angulimalya were a sect or set of Sivaitic fanatics, who made assassination a religious act. The one of them here mentioned had joined them by the force of circumstances. Being converted by Buddha, he became a monk; but when it is said in the text that he "got the Tao," or doctrine, I

73

think that expression implies more than his conversion, and is equivalent to his becoming an Arhat. His name in Pali is Angulimala. That he did become an Arhat is clear from his autobiographical poem in the "Songs of the Theras."

[7] Eitel (p. 37) says:--"A noted vihara in the suburbs of Sravasti, erected in a park which Anatha-pindika bought of prince Jeta, the son of Prasenajit. Sakyamuni made this place his favourite residence for many years. Most of the Sutras (authentic and supposititious) date from this spot."

[8] See chapter xvii.

[9] See chapter xiii.

[10] Arya, meaning "honourable," "venerable," is a title given only to those who have mastered the four spiritual truths:--(1) that "misery" is a necessary condition of all sentient existence; this is duhkha: (2) that the "accumulation" of misery is caused by the passions; this is samudaya: (3) that the "extinction" of passion is possible; this is nirodha: and (4) that the "path" leads to the extinction of passion; which is marga. According to their attainment of these truths, the Aryas, or followers of Buddha, are distinguished into four classes,-- Srotapannas, Sakridagamins, Anagamins, and Arhats. E. H., p. 14.

[11] This is the first time that Fa-hien employs the name Ho-shang {.} {.}, which is now popularly used in China for all Buddhist monks without distinction of rank or office. It is the representative of the Sanskrit term Upadhyaya, "explained," says Eitel (p. 155) by "a self-taught teacher," or by "he who knows what is sinful and what is not sinful," with the note, "In India the vernacular of this term is {.} {.} (? munshee [? Bronze]); in Kustana and Kashgar they say {.} {.} (hwa-shay); and from the latter term are derived the Chinese synonyms, {.} {.} (ho-shay) and {.} {.} (ho-shang)." The Indian term was originally a designation for those who teach only a part of the Vedas, the Vedangas. Adopted by Buddhists of Central Asia, it was made to signify the priests of the older ritual, in distinction from the Lamas. In China it has been used first as a synonym for {.} {.}, monks engaged in popular

teaching (teachers of the Law), in distinction from {.} {.}, disciplinists, and {.} {.}, contemplative philosophers (meditationists); then it was used to designate the abbots of monasteries. But it is now popularly applied to all Buddhist monks. In the text there seems to be implied some distinction between the "teachers" and the "ho-shang;"--probably, the Pali Akariya and Upagghaya; see Sacred Books of the East, vol. xiii, Vinaya Texts, pp. 178, 179.

[12] It might be added, "as depending on it," in order to bring out the full meaning of the {.} in the text. If I recollect aright, the help of the police had to be called in at Hong Kong in its early years, to keep the approaches to the Cathedral free from the number of beggars, who squatted down there during service, hoping that the hearers would come out with softened hearts, and disposed to be charitable. I found the popular tutelary temples in Peking and other places, and the path up Mount T'ai in Shan-lung similarly frequented.

[13] The wife of Anatha-pindika, and who became "mother superior" of many nunneries. See her history in M. B., pp. 220-227. I am surprised it does not end with the statement that she is to become a Buddha.

[14] See E. H., p. 136. Hsuan-chwang does not give the name of this murderer; see in Julien's "Vie et Voyages de Hiouen-thsang," p. 125,-- "a heretical Brahman killed a woman and calumniated Buddha." See also the fuller account in Beal's "Records of Western Countries," pp. 7, 8, where the murder is committed by several Brahmacharins. In this passage Beal makes Sundari to be the name of the murdered person (a harlot). But the text cannot be so construed.

[15] Eitel (p. 144) calls her Chancha; in Singhalese, Chinchi. See the story about her, M. B., pp. 275-277.

[16] "Earth's prison," or "one of Earth's prisons." It was the Avichi naraka to which she went, the last of the eight hot prisons, where the culprits die, and are born again in uninterrupted succession (such being the meaning of Avichi), though not without hope of final redemption. E. H. p. 21.

[17] Devadatta was brother of Ananda, and a near relative therefore of Sakyamuni. He was the deadly enemy, however, of the latter. He had become so in an earlier state of existence, and the hatred continued in every successive birth, through which they reappeared in the world. See the accounts of him, and of his various devices against Buddha, and his own destruction at the last, in M. B., pp. 315-321, 326-330; and still better, in the Sacred Books of the East, vol. xx, Vinaya Texts, pp. 233-265. For the particular attempt referred to in the text, see "The Life of the Buddha," p. 107. When he was engulphed, and the flames were around him, he cried out to Buddha to save him, and we are told that he is expected yet to appear as a Buddha under the name of Devaraja, in a universe called Deva-soppana. E. H., p. 39.

[18] "A devalaya ({.} {.} or {.} {.}), a place in which a deva is worshipped,--a general name for all Brahmanical temples" (Eitel, p. 30). We read in the Khang-hsi dictionary under {.}, that when Kasyapa Matanga came to the Western Regions, with his Classics or Sutras, he was lodged in the Court of State-Ceremonial, and that afterwards there was built for him "The Court of the White-horse" ({.} {.} {.}), and in consequence the name of Sze {.} came to be given to all Buddhistic temples. Fa-hien, however, applies this term only to Brahmanical temples.

[19] Their speech was somewhat unconnected, but natural enough in the circumstances. Compare the whole account with the narrative in I Samuel v. about the Ark and Dagon, that "twice-battered god of Palestine."

[20] "Entered the doctrine or path." Three stages in the Buddhistic life are indicated by Fa-hien:--"entering it," as here, by becoming monks ({.} {.}); "getting it," by becoming Arhats ({.} {.}); and "completing it," by becoming Buddha ({.} {.}).

[21] It is not quite clear whether the author had in mind here Central India as a whole, which I think he had, or only Kosala, the part of it where he then was. In the older teaching, there were only thirty-two sects, but there may have been three subdivisions of each. See Rhys Davids' "Buddhism," pp. 98, 99.

[22] This mention of "the future world" is an important difference between the Corean and Chinese texts. The want of it in the latter has been a stumbling-block in the way of all previous translators. Remusat says in a note that "the heretics limited themselves to speak of the duties of man in his actual life without connecting it by the notion that the metempsychosis with the anterior periods of existence through which he had passed." But this is just the opposite of what Fa-hien's meaning was, according to our Corean text. The notion of "the metempsychosis" was just that in which all the ninety-six erroneous systems agreed among themselves and with Buddhism. If he had wished to say what the French sinologue thinks he does say, moreover, he would probably have written {.} {.} {.} {.} {.}. Let me add, however, that the connexion which Buddhism holds between the past world (including the present) and the future is not that of a metempsychosis, or transmigration of souls, for it does not appear to admit any separate existence of the soul. Adhering to its own phraseology of "the wheel," I would call its doctrine that of "The Transrotation of Births." See Rhys Davids' third Hibbert Lecture.

[23] Or, more according to the phonetisation of the text, Vaidurya. He was king of Kosala, the son and successor of Prasenajit, and the destroyer of Kapilavastu, the city of the Sakya family. His hostility to the Sakyas is sufficiently established, and it may be considered as certain that the name Shay-e, which, according to Julien's "Methode," p. 89, may be read Chia-e, is the same as Kia-e ({.} {.}), one of the phonetisations of Kapilavastu, as given by Eitel.

[24] This would be the interview in the "Life of the Buddha" in Trubner's Oriental Series, p. 116, when Virudhaha on his march found Buddha under an old sakotato tree. It afforded him no shade; but he told the king that the thought of the danger of "his relatives and kindred made it shady." The king was moved to sympathy for the time, and went back to Sravasti; but the destruction of Kapilavastu was only postponed for a short space, and Buddha himself acknowledged it to be inevitable in the connexion of cause and effect.

CHAPTER XXI

THE THREE PREDECESSORS OF SAKYAMUNI IN THE BUDDHASHIP.

Fifty le to the west of the city bring (the traveller) to a town named Too-wei,[1] the birthplace of Kasyapa Buddha.[1] At the place where he and his father met,[2] and at that where he attained to pari-nirvana, topes were erected. Over the entire relic of the whole body of him, the Kasyapa Tathagata,[3] a great tope was also erected.

Going on south-east from the city of Sravasti for twelve yojanas, (the travellers) came to a town named Na-pei-kea,[4] the birthplace of Krakuchanda Buddha. At the place where he and his father met, and at that where he attained to pari-nirvana, topes were erected. Going north from here less than a yojana, they came to a town which had been the birthplace of Kanakamuni Buddha. At the place where he and his father met, and where he attained to pari-nirvana, topes were erected.

NOTES

[1] Identified, as Beal says, by Cunningham with Tadwa, a village nine miles to the west of Sahara-mahat. The birthplace of Kasyapa Buddha is generally thought to have been Benares. According to a calculation of Remusat, from his birth to A.D. 1832 there were 1,992,859 years!

[2] It seems to be necessary to have a meeting between every Buddha and his father. One at least is ascribed to Sakyamuni and his father (real or supposed) Suddhodana.

[3] This is the highest epithet given to every supreme Buddha; in Chinese {.} {.}, meaning, as Eitel, p. 147 says, "/Sic profectus sum/." It is equivalent to "Rightful Buddha, the true successor in the Supreme Buddha Line." Hardy concludes his account of the Kasyapa Buddha (M. B., p. 97) with the following sentence:--"After his body was burnt, the bones still remained in their usual position, presenting the appearance of a perfect skeleton; and the

78

whole of the inhabitants of Jambudvipa, assembling together, erected a dagoba over his relics one yojana in height!"

[4] Na-pei-kea or Nabhiga is not mentioned elsewhere. Eitel says this Buddha was born at the city of Gan-ho ({.} {.} {.}) and Hardy gives his birthplace as Mekhala. It may be possible, by means of Sanskrit, to reconcile these statements.

CHAPTER XXII

KAPILAVASTU. ITS DESOLATION. LEGENDS OF BUDDHA'S BIRTH, AND OTHER INCIDENTS IN CONNEXION WITH IT.

Less than a yojana to the east from this brought them to the city of Kapilavastu;[1] but in it there was neither king nor people. All was mound and desolation. Of inhabitants there were only some monks and a score or two of families of the common people. At the spot where stood the old palace of king Suddhodana[2] there have been made images of the prince (his eldest son) and his mother;[3] and at the places where that son appeared mounted on a white elephant when he entered his mother's womb,[4] and where he turned his carriage round on seeing the sick man after he had gone out of the city by the eastern gate,[5] topes have been erected. The places (were also pointed out)[6] where (the rishi) A-e[7] inspected the marks (of Buddhaship on the body) of the heir-apparent (when an infant); where, when he was in company with Nanda and others, on the elephant being struck down and drawn to one side, he tossed it away;[8] where he shot an arrow to the south-east, and it went a distance of thirty le, then entering the ground and making a spring to come forth, which men subsequently fashioned into a well from which travellers might drink;[9] where, after he had attained to Wisdom, Buddha returned and saw the king, his father;[10] where five hundred Sakyas quitted their families and did reverence to Upali[11] while the earth shook and moved in six different ways; where Buddha preached his Law to the devas, and the four deva kings and others kept the four doors (of the hall), so that (even) the king, his father, could not enter;[12] where Buddha sat under a nyagrodha tree, which is still standing,[13] with his face to the east, and (his aunt) Maja-prajapati presented him with a Sanghali;[14]

and (where) king Vaidurya slew the seed of Sakya, and they all in dying became Srotapannas.[15] A tope was erected at this last place, which is still existing.

Several le north-east from the city was the king's field, where the heir-apparent sat under a tree, and looked at the ploughers.[16]

Fifty le east from the city was a garden, named Lumbini,[17] where the queen entered the pond and bathed. Having come forth from the pond on the northern bank, after (walking) twenty paces, she lifted up her hand, laid hold of a branch of a tree, and, with her face to the east, gave birth to the heir-apparent.[18] When he fell to the ground, he (immediately) walked seven paces. Two dragon-kings (appeared) and washed his body. At the place where they did so, there was immediately formed a well, and from it, as well as from the above pond, where (the queen) bathed,[19] the monks (even) now constantly take the water, and drink it.

There are four places of regular and fixed occurrence (in the history of) all Buddhas:--first, the place where they attained to perfect Wisdom (and became Buddha); second, the place where they turned the wheel of the Law;[20] third, the place where they preached the Law, discoursed of righteousness, and discomfited (the advocates of) erroneous doctrines; and fourth, the place where they came down, after going up to the Trayatrimsas heaven to preach the Law for the benefit of their mothers. Other places in connexion with them became remarkable, according to the manifestations which were made at them at particular times.

The country of Kapilavastu is a great scene of empty desolation. The inhabitants are few and far between. On the roads people have to be on their guard against white elephants[21] and lions, and should not travel incautiously.

NOTES

[1] Kapilavastu, "the city of beautiful virtue," was the birthplace of Sakyamuni, but was destroyed, as intimated in the notes on last chapter,

during his lifetime. It was situated a short distance north- west of the present Goruckpoor, lat. 26d 46s N., lon. 83d 19s E. Davids says (Manual, p. 25), "It was on the banks of the river Rohini, the modern Kohana, about 100 miles north-west of the city of Benares."

[2] The father, or supposed father, of Sakyamuni. He is here called "the king white and pure" ({.} {.} {.}). A more common appellation is "the king of pure rice" ({.} {.} {.});" but the character {.}, or "rice," must be a mistake for {.}, "Brahman," and the appellation= "Pure Brahman king."

[3] The "eldest son," or "prince" was Sakyamuni, and his mother had no other son. For "his mother," see chap. xvii, note 3. She was a daughter of Anjana or Anusakya, king of the neighbouring country of Koli, and Yasodhara, an aunt of Suddhodana. There appear to have been various intermarriages between the royal houses of Kapila and Koli.

[4] In "The Life of the Buddha," p. 15, we read that "Buddha was now in the Tushita heaven, and knowing that his time was come (the time for his last rebirth in the course of which he would become Buddha), he made the necessary examinations; and having decided that Maha-maya was the right mother, in the midnight watch he entered her womb under the appearance of an elephant." See M. B., pp. 140-143, and, still better, Rhys Davids' "Birth Stories," pp. 58-63.

[5] In Hardy's M. B., pp. 154, 155, we read, "As the prince (Siddhartha, the first name given to Sakyamuni; see Eitel, under Sarvarthasiddha) was one day passing along, he saw a deva under the appearance of a leper, full of sores, with a body like a water-vessel, and legs like the pestle for pounding rice; and when he learned from his charioteer what it was that he saw, be became agitated, and returned at once to the palace." See also Rhys Davids' "Buddhism," p. 29.

[6] This is an addition of my own, instead of "There are also topes erected at the following spots," of former translators. Fa-hien does not say that there were memorial topes at all these places.

[7] Asita; see Eitel, p. 15. He is called in Pali Kala Devala, and had been a minister of Suddhodana's father.

[8] In "The Life of Buddha" we read that the Lichchhavis of Vaisali had sent to the young prince a very fine elephant; but when it was near Kapilavastu, Devadatta, out of envy, killed it with a blow of his fist. Nanda (not Ananda, but a half-brother of Siddhartha), coming that way, saw the carcase lying on the road, and pulled it on one side; but the Bodhisattva, seeing it there, took it by the tail, and tossed it over seven fences and ditches, when the force of its fall made a great ditch. I suspect that the characters in the column have been disarranged, and that we should read {.} {.} {.} {.}, {.} {.}, {.} {.}. Buddha, that is Siddhartha, was at this time only ten years old.

[9] The young Sakyas were shooting when the prince thus surpassed them all. He was then seventeen.

[10] This was not the night when he finally fled from Kapilavastu, and as he was leaving the palace, perceiving his sleeping father, and said, "Father, though I love thee, yet a fear possesses me, and I may not stay;"--The Life of the Buddha, p. 25. Most probably it was that related in M. B., pp. 199-204. See "Buddhist Birth Stories," pp. 120- 127.

[11] They did this, I suppose, to show their humility, for Upali was only a Sudra by birth, and had been a barber; so from the first did Buddhism assert its superiority to the conditions of rank and caste. Upali was distinguished by his knowledge of the rules of discipline, and praised on that account by Buddha. He was one of the three leaders of the first synod, and the principal compiler of the original Vinaya books.

[12] I have not met with the particulars of this preaching.

[13] Meaning, as explained in Chinese, "a tree without knots;" the /ficus Indica/. See Rhys Davids' note, Manual, p. 39, where he says that a branch of one of these trees was taken from Buddha Gaya to Anuradhapura in Ceylon in the middle of the third century B.C, and is still growing there, the oldest historical tree in the world.

[14] See chap. xiii, note 11. I have not met with the account of this presentation. See the long account of Prajapati in M. B., pp. 306-315.

[15] See chap. xx, note 10. The Srotapannas are the first class of saints, who are not to be reborn in a lower sphere, but attain to nirvana after having been reborn seven times consecutively as men or devas. The Chinese editions state there were "1000" of the Sakya seed. The general account is that they were 500, all maidens, who refused to take their place in king Vaidurya's harem, and were in consequence taken to a pond, and had their hands and feet cut off. There Buddha came to them, had their wounds dressed, and preached to them the Law. They died in the faith, and were reborn in the region of the four Great Kings. Thence they came back and visited Buddha at Jetavana in the night, and there they obtained the reward of Srotapanna. "The Life of the Buddha," p. 121.

[16] See the account of this event in M. B., p. 150. The account of it reminds me of the ploughing by the sovereign, which has been an institution in China from the earliest times. But there we have no magic and no extravagance.

[17] "The place of Liberation;" see chap. xiii, note 7.

[18] See the accounts of this event in M. B., pp. 145, 146; "The Life of the Buddha," pp. 15, 16; and "Buddhist Birth Stories," p. 66.

[19] There is difficulty in construing the text of this last statement. Mr. Beal had, no doubt inadvertently, omitted it in his first translation. In his revised version he gives for it, I cannot say happily, "As well as at the pool, the water of which came down from above for washing (the child)."

[20] See chap. xvii, note 8. See also Davids' Manual, p. 45. The latter says, that "to turn the wheel of the Law" means "to set rolling the royal chariot wheel of a universal empire of truth and righteousness;" but he admits that this is more grandiloquent than the phraseology was in the ears of Buddhists. I prefer the words quoted from Eitel in the note referred to. "They turned" is

probably equivalent to "They began to turn."

[21] Fa-hien does not say that he himself saw any of these white elephants, nor does he speak of the lions as of any particular colour. We shall find by-and-by, in a note further on, that, to make them appear more terrible, they are spoken of as "black."

CHAPTER XXIII

RAMA, AND ITS TOPE.

East from Buddha's birthplace, and at a distance of five yojanas, there is a kingdom called Rama.[1] The king of this country, having obtained one portion of the relics of Buddha's body,[2] returned with it and built over it a tope, named the Rama tope. By the side of it there was a pool, and in the pool a dragon, which constantly kept watch over (the tope), and presented offerings to it day and night. When king Asoka came forth into the world, he wished to destroy the eight topes (over the relics), and to build (instead of them) 84,000 topes.[3] After he had thrown down the seven (others), he wished next to destroy this tope. But then the dragon showed itself, took the king into its palace;[4] and when he had seen all the things provided for offerings, it said to him, "If you are able with your offerings to exceed these, you can destroy the tope, and take it all away. I will not contend with you." The king, however, knew that such appliances for offerings were not to be had anywhere in the world, and thereupon returned (without carrying out his purpose).

(Afterwards), the ground all about became overgrown with vegetation, and there was nobody to sprinkle and sweep (about the tope); but a herd of elephants came regularly, which brought water with their trunks to water the ground, and various kinds of flowers and incense, which they presented at the tope. (Once) there came from one of the kingdoms a devotee[5] to worship at the tope. When he encountered the elephants he was greatly alarmed, and screened himself among the trees; but when he saw them go through with the offerings in the most proper manner, the thought filled him with great sadness--that there should be no monastery here, (the inmates of

84

which) might serve the tope, but the elephants have to do the watering and sweeping. Forthwith he gave up the great prohibitions (by which he was bound),[6] and resumed the status of a Sramanera.[7] With his own hands he cleared away the grass and trees, put the place in good order, and made it pure and clean. By the power of his exhortations, he prevailed on the king of the country to form a residence for monks; and when that was done, he became head of the monastery. At the present day there are monks residing in it. This event is of recent occurrence; but in all the succession from that time till now, there has always been a Sramanera head of the establishment.

NOTES

[1] Rama or Ramagrama, between Kapilavastu and Kusanagara.

[2] See the account of the eightfold division of the relics of Buddha's body in the Sacred Books of the East, vol. xi, Buddhist Suttas, pp. 133-136.

[3] The bones of the human body are supposed to consist of 84,000 atoms, and hence the legend of Asoka's wish to build 84,000 topes, one over each atom of Sakyamuni's skeleton.

[4] Fa-hien, it appears to me, intended his readers to understand that the naga-guardian had a palace of his own, inside or underneath the pool or tank.

[5] It stands out on the narrative as a whole that we have not here "some pilgrims," but one devotee.

[6] What the "great prohibitions" which the devotee now gave up were we cannot tell. Being what he was, a monk of more than ordinary ascetical habits, he may have undertaken peculiar and difficult vows.

[7] The Sramanera, or in Chinese Shamei. See chap. xvi, note 19.

CHAPTER XXIV

WHERE BUDDHA FINALLY RENOUNCED THE WORLD, AND

WHERE HE DIED.

East from here four yojanas, there is the place where the heir- apparent sent back Chandaka, with his white horse;[1] and there also a tope was erected.

Four yojanas to the east from this, (the travellers) came to the Charcoal tope,[2] where there is also a monastery.

Going on twelve yojanas, still to the east, they came to the city of Kusanagara,[3] on the north of which, between two trees,[4] on the bank of the Nairanjana[5] river, is the place where the World-honoured one, with his head to the north, attained to pari-nirvana (and died). There also are the places where Subhadra,[6] the last (of his converts), attained to Wisdom (and became an Arhat); where in his coffin of gold they made offerings to the World-honoured one for seven days,[7] where the Vajrapani laid aside his golden club,[8] and where the eight kings[9] divided the relics (of the burnt body):--at all these places were built topes and monasteries, all of which are now existing.

In the city the inhabitants are few and far between, comprising only the families belonging to the (different) societies of monks.

Going from this to the south-east for twelve yojanas, they came to the place where the Lichchhavis[10] wished to follow Buddha to (the place of) his pari-nirvana, and where, when he would not listen to them and they kept cleaving to him, unwilling to go away, he made to appear a large and deep ditch which they could not cross over, and gave them his alms-bowl, as a pledge of his regard, (thus) sending them back to their families. There a stone pillar was erected with an account of this event engraved upon it.

NOTES

[1] This was on the night when Sakyamuni finally left his palace and family to fulfil the course to which he felt that he was called. Chandaka, in Pali Channa, was the prince's charioteer, and in sympathy with him. So also was the white horse Kanthaka (Kanthakanam Asvaraja), which neighed his

delight till the devas heard him. See M. B., pp. 158-161, and Davids' Manual, pp. 32, 33. According to "Buddhist Birth Stories," p. 87, the noble horse never returned to the city, but died of grief at being left by his master, to be reborn immediately in the Trayastrimsas heaven as the deva Kanthaka!

[2] Beal and Giles call this the "Ashes" tope. I also would have preferred to call it so; but the Chinese character is {.}, not {.}. Remusat has "la tour des charbons." It was over the place of Buddha's cremation.

[3] In Pali Kusinara. It got its name from the Kusa grass (the /poa cynosuroides/); and its ruins are still extant, near Kusiah, 180 N.W. from Patna; "about," says Davids, "120 miles N.N.E. of Benares, and 80 miles due east of Kapilavastu."

[4] The Sala tree, the /Shorea robusta/, which yields the famous teak wood.

[5] Confounded, according to Eitel, even by Hsuan-chwang, with the Hiranyavati, which flows past the city on the south.

[6] A Brahman of Benares, said to have been 120 years old, who came to learn from Buddha the very night he died. Ananda would have repulsed him; but Buddha ordered him to be introduced; and then putting aside the ingenious but unimportant question which he propounded, preached to him the Law. The Brahman was converted and attained at once to Arhatship. Eitel says that he attained to nirvana a few moments before Sakyamuni; but see the full account of him and his conversion in "Buddhist Suttas," p. 103-110.

[7] Thus treating the dead Buddha as if he had been a Chakravartti king. Hardy's M. B., p. 347, says:--"For the place of cremation, the princes (of Kusinara) offered their own coronation-hall, which was decorated with the utmost magnificence, and the body was deposited in a golden sarcophagus." See the account of a cremation which Fa-hien witnessed in Ceylon, chap. xxxix.

[8] The name Vajrapani is explained as "he who holds in his hand the

diamond club (or pestle=sceptre)," which is one of the many names of Indra or Sakra. He therefore, that great protector of Buddhism, would seem to be intended here; but the difficulty with me is that neither in Hardy nor Rockhill, nor any other writer, have I met with any manifestation of himself made by Indra on this occasion. The princes of Kusanagara were called mallas, "strong or mighty heroes;" so also were those of Pava and Vaisali; and a question arises whether the language may not refer to some story which Fa-hien had heard,-- something which they did on this great occasion. Vajrapani is also explained as meaning "the diamond mighty hero;" but the epithet of "diamond" is not so applicable to them as to Indra. The clause may hereafter obtain more elucidation.

[9] Of Kusanagara, Pava, Vaisali, and other kingdoms. Kings, princes, brahmans,--each wanted the whole relic; but they agreed to an eightfold division at the suggestion of the brahman Drona.

[10] These "strong heroes" were the chiefs of Vaisali, a kingdom and city, with an oligarchical constitution. They embraced Buddhism early, and were noted for their peculiar attachment to Buddha. The second synod was held at Vaisali, as related in the next chapter. The ruins of the city still exist at Bassahar, north of Patna, the same, I suppose, as Besarh, twenty miles north of Hajipur. See Beal's Revised Version, p. lii.

CHAPTER XXV

VAISALI. THE TOPE CALLED "WEAPONS LAID DOWN." THE COUNCIL OF VAISALI.

East from this city ten yojanas, (the travellers) came to the kingdom of Vaisali. North of the city so named is a large forest, having in it the double-galleried vihara[1] where Buddha dwelt, and the tope over half the body of Ananda.[2] Inside the city the woman Ambapali[3] built a vihara in honour of Buddha, which is now standing as it was at first. Three le south of the city, on the west of the road, (is the) garden (which) the same Ambapali presented to Buddha, in which he might reside. When Buddha was about to attain to his pari-nirvana, as he was quitting the city by the west gate, he turned round, and, beholding the city on his right, said to them, "Here I have taken my last walk."[4] Men subsequently built a tope at this spot.

Three le north-west of the city there is a tope called, "Bows and weapons laid down." The reason why it got that name was this:--The inferior wife of a king, whose country lay along the river Ganges, brought forth from her womb a ball of flesh. The superior wife, jealous of the other, said, "You have brought forth a thing of evil omen," and immediately it was put into a box of wood and thrown into the river. Farther down the stream another king was walking and looking about, when he saw the wooden box (floating) in the water. (He had it brought to him), opened it, and found a thousand little boys, upright and complete, and each one different from the others. He took them and had them brought up. They grew tall and large, and very daring, and strong, crushing all opposition in every expedition which they undertook. By and by they attacked the kingdom of their real father, who became in consequence greatly distressed and sad. His inferior wife asked what it was that made him so, and he replied, "That king has a thousand sons, daring and strong beyond compare, and he wishes with them to attack my kingdom; this is what makes me sad." The wife said, "You need not be sad and sorrowful. Only make a high gallery on the wall of the city on the east; and when the thieves come, I shall be able to make them retire." The king did as she said; and when the enemies came, she said to them from the tower, "You are my sons; why are you acting so unnaturally and rebelliously?" They replied, "If you do not believe me," she said, "look, all of you, towards me, and open your mouths." She then pressed her breasts with her two hands, and each sent forth 500 jets of milk, which fell into the mouths of the thousand sons. The thieves (thus) knew that she was their mother, and laid down their bows and weapons.[5] The two kings, the fathers, thereupon fell into reflection, and both got to be Pratyeka Buddhas.[6] The tope of the two Pratyeka Buddhas is still existing.

In a subsequent age, when the World-honoured one had attained to perfect Wisdom (and become Buddha), he said to is disciples, "This is the place where I in a former age laid down my bow and weapons."[7] It was thus that subsequently men got to know (the fact), and raised the tope on this spot, which in this way received its name. The thousand little boys were the thousand Buddhas of this Bhadra-kalpa.[8]

It was by the side of the "Weapons-laid-down" tope that Buddha, having given up the idea of living longer, said to Ananda, "In three months from this I will attain to pavi-nirvana;" and king Mara[9] had so fascinated and stupefied Ananda, that he was not able to ask Buddha to remain longer in this world.

Three or four le east from this place there is a tope (commemorating the following occurrence):--A hundred years after the pari-nirvana of Buddha, some Bhikshus of Vaisali went wrong in the matter of the disciplinary rules in ten particulars, and appealed for their justification to what they said were the words of Buddha. Hereupon the Arhats and Bhikshus observant of the rules, to the number in all of 700 monks, examined afresh and collated the collection of disciplinary books.[10] Subsequently men built at this place the tope (in question), which is still existing.

NOTES

[1] It is difficult to tell what was the peculiar form of this vihara from which it gets its name; something about the construction of its door, or cupboards, or galleries.

[2] See the explanation of this in the next chapter.

[3] Ambapali, Amrapali, or Amradarika, "the guardian of the Amra (probably the mango) tree," is famous in Buddhist annals. See the account of her in M. B., pp. 456-8. She was a courtesan. She had been in many narakas or hells, was 100,000 times a female beggar, and 10,000 times a prostitute; but maintaining perfect continence during the period of Kasyapa Buddha, Sakyamuni's predecessor, she had been born a devi, and finally appeared in earth under an Amra tree in Vaisali. There again she fell into her old ways, and had a son by king Bimbisara; but she was won over by Buddha to virtue and chastity, renounced the world, and attained to the state of an Arhat. See the earliest account of Ambapali's presentation of the garden in "Buddhist Suttas," pp. 30-33, and the note there from Bishop Bigandet on pp. 33, 34.

[4] Beal gives, "In this place I have performed the last religious act of my earthly career;" Giles, "This is the last place I shall visit;" Remusat, "C'est un lieu ou je reviendrai bien longtemps apres ceci." Perhaps the "walk" to which Buddha referred had been for meditation.

[5] See the account of this legend in the note in M. B., pp. 235, 236, different, but not less absurd. The first part of Fa-hien's narrative will have sent the thoughts of some of my readers to the exposure of the infant Moses, as related in Exodus. [Certainly did.--JB.]

[6] See chap. xiii, note 14.

[7] Thus Sakyamuni had been one of the thousand little boys who floated in the box in the Ganges. How long back the former age was we cannot tell. I suppose the tope of the two fathers who became Pratyeka Buddhas had been built like the one commemorating the laying down of weapons after Buddha had told his disciples of the strange events in the past.

[8] Bhadra-kalpa, "the Kalpa of worthies or sages." "This," says Eitel, p. 22, "is a designation for a Kalpa of stability, so called because 1000 Buddhas appear in the course of it. Our present period is a Bhadra-kalpa, and four Buddhas have already appeared. It is to last 236 million years, but over 151 millions have already elapsed."

[9] "The king of demons." The name Mara is explained by "the murderer," "the destroyer of virtue," and similar appellations. "He is," says Eitel, "the personification of lust, the god of love, sin, and death, the arch-enemy of goodness, residing in the heaven Paranirmita Vasavartin on the top of the Kamadhatu. He assumes different forms, especially monstrous ones, to tempt or frighten the saints, or sends his daughters, or inspires wicked men like Devadatta or the Nirgranthas to do his work. He is often represented with 100 arms, and riding on an elephant." The oldest form of the legend in this paragraph is in "Buddhist Suttas," Sacred Books of the East, vol. xi, pp. 41-55, where Buddha says that, if Ananda had asked him thrice, he would have postponed his death.

[10] Or the Vinaya-pitaka. The meeting referred to was an important one, and is generally spoken of as the second Great Council of the Buddhist Church. See, on the formation of the Buddhist Canon, Hardy's E. M., chap. xviii, and the last chapter of Davids' Manual, on the History of the Order. The first Council was that held at Rajagriha, shortly after Buddha's death, under the presidency of Kasyapa;--say about B.C. 410. The second was that spoken of here;--say about B.C. 300. In Davids' Manual (p. 216) we find the ten points of discipline, in which the heretics (I can use that term here) claimed at least indulgence. Two meetings were held to consider and discuss them. At the former the orthodox party barely succeeded in carrying their condemnation of the laxer monks; and a second and larger meeting, of which Fa-hien speaks, was held in consequence, and a more emphatic condemnation passed. At the same time all the books and subjects of discipline seem to have undergone a careful revision.

The Corean text is clearer than the Chinese as to those who composed the Council,--the Arhats and orthodox monks. The leader among them was a Yasas, or Yasada, or Yedsaputtra, who had been a disciple of Ananda, and must therefore have been a very old man.

CHAPTER XXVI

REMARKABLE DEATH OF ANANDA.

Four yojanas on from this place to the east brought the travellers to the confluence of the five rivers.[1] When Ananda was going from Magadha[2] to Vaisali, wishing his pari-nirvana to take place (there), the devas informed king Ajatasatru[3] of it, and the king immediately pursued him, in his own grand carriage, with a body of soldiers, and had reached the river. (On the other hand), the Lichchhavis of Vaisali had heard that Amanda was coming (to their city), and they on their part came to meet him. (In this way), they all arrived together at the river, and Ananda considered that, if he went forward, king Ajatasatru would be very angry, while, if he went back, the Lichchhavis would resent his conduct. He thereupon in the very middle of the river burnt his body in a fiery ecstasy of Samadhi,[4] and his pari-nirvana was attained.

He divided his body (also) into two, (leaving) the half of it on each bank; so that each of the two kings got one half as a (sacred) relic, and took it back (to his own capital), and there raised a tope over it.

NOTES

[1] This spot does not appear to have been identified. It could not be far from Patna.

[2] Magadha was for some time the headquarters of Buddhism; the holy land, covered with viharas; a fact perpetuated, as has been observed in a previous note, in the name of the present Behar, the southern portion of which corresponds to the ancient kingdom of Magadha.

[3] In Singhalese, Ajasat. See the account of his conversion in M. B., pp. 321-326. He was the son of king Bimbisara, who was one of the first royal converts to Buddhism. Ajasat murdered his father, or at least wrought his death; and was at first opposed to Sakyamuni, and a favourer of Devadatta. When converted, he became famous for his liberality in almsgiving.

[4] Eitel has a long article (pp. 114, 115) on the meaning of Samadhi, which is one of the seven sections of wisdom (bodhyanga). Hardy defines it as meaning "perfect tranquillity;" Turnour, as "meditative abstraction;" Burnouf, as "self-control;" and Edkins, as "ecstatic reverie." "Samadhi," says Eitel, "signifies the highest pitch of abstract, ecstatic meditation; a state of absolute indifference to all influences from within or without; a state of torpor of both the material and spiritual forces of vitality; a sort of terrestrial nirvana, consistently culminating in total destruction of life." He then quotes apparently the language of the text, "He consumed his body by Agni (the fire of) Samadhi," and says it is "a common expression for the effects of such ecstatic, ultra-mystic self-annihilation." All this is simply "a darkening of counsel by words without knowledge." Some facts concerning the death of Ananda are hidden beneath the darkness of the phraseology, which it is impossible for us to ascertain. By or in Samadhi he burns his body in the very middle of the river, and then he divides the relic of the burnt body into two parts (for so evidently Fa-hien intended his narration to be taken), and

93

leaves one half on each bank. The account of Ananda's death in Nien-ch'ang's "History of Buddha and the Patriarchs" is much more extravagant. Crowds of men and devas are brought together to witness it. The body is divided into four parts. One is conveyed to the Tushita heaven; a second, to the palace of a certain Naga king; a third is given to Ajatasatru; and the fourth to the Lichchhavis. What it all really means I cannot tell.

CHAPTER XXVII

PATALIPUTTRA OR PATNA, IN MAGADHA. KING ASOKA'S SPIRIT-BUILT PALACE AND HALLS. THE BUDDHIST BRAHMAN, RADHA-SAMI. DISPENSARIES AND HOSPITALS.

Having crossed the river, and descended south for a yojana, (the travellers) came to the town of Pataliputtra,[1] in the kingdom of Magadha, the city where king Asoka[2] ruled. The royal palace and halls in the midst of the city, which exist now as of old, were all made by spirits which he employed, and which piled up the stones, reared the walls and gates, and executed the elegant carving and inlaid sculpture-work,--in a way which no human hands of this world could accomplish.

King Asoka had a younger brother who had attained to be an Arhat, and resided on Gridhra-kuta[3] hill, finding his delight in solitude and quiet. The king, who sincerely reverenced him, wished and begged him (to come and live) in his family, where he could supply all his wants. The other, however, through his delight in the stillness of the mountain, was unwilling to accept the invitation, on which the king said to him, "Only accept my invitation, and I will make a hill for you inside the city." Accordingly, he provided the materials of a feast, called to him the spirits, and announced to them, "To-morrow you will all receive my invitation; but as there are no mats for you to sit on, let each one bring (his own seat)." Next day the spirits came, each one bringing with him a great rock, (like) a wall, four or five paces square, (for a seat). When their sitting was over, the king made them form a hill with the large stones piled on one another, and also at the foot of the hill, with five large square stones, to make an apartment, which might be more than thirty cubits long, twenty cubits wide, and more than ten cubits high.

In this city there had resided a great Brahman,[4] named Radha- sami,[5] a professor of the mahayana, of clear discernment and much wisdom, who understood everything, living by himself in spotless purity. The king of the country honoured and reverenced him, and served him as his teacher. If he went to inquire for and greet him, the king did not presume to sit down alongside of him; and if, in his love and reverence, he took hold of his hand, as soon as he let it go, the Brahman made haste to pour water on it and wash it. He might be more than fifty years old, and all the kingdom looked up to him. By means of this one man, the Law of Buddha was widely made known, and the followers of other doctrines did not find it in their power to persecute the body of monks in any way.

By the side of the tope of Asoka, there has been made a mahayana monastery, very grand and beautiful; there is also a hinayana one; the two together containing six or seven hundred monks. The rules of demeanour and the scholastic arrangements[6] in them are worthy of observation.

Shamans of the highest virtue from all quarters, and students, inquirers wishing to find out truth and the grounds of it, all resort to these monasteries. There also resides in this monastery a Brahman teacher, whose name also is Manjusri,[7] whom the Shamans of greatest virtue in the kingdom, and the mahayana Bhikshus honour and look up to.

The cities and towns of this country are the greatest of all in the Middle Kingdom. The inhabitants are rich and prosperous, and vie with one another in the practice of benevolence and righteousness. Every year on the eighth day of the second month they celebrate a procession of images. They make a four-wheeled car, and on it erect a structure of four storeys by means of bamboos tied together. This is supported by a king-post, with poles and lances slanting from it, and is rather more than twenty cubits high, having the shape of a tope. White and silk-like cloth of hair[8] is wrapped all round it, which is then painted in various colours. They make figures of devas, with gold, silver, and lapis lazuli grandly blended and having silken streamers and canopies hung out over them. On the four sides are niches, with a Buddha seated in each, and a Bodhisattva standing in attendance on him. There may be twenty cars, all grand and imposing, but each one different from the others. On the day mentioned, the monks and laity within the borders all come together; they have singers and skilful musicians; they pay their devotion with flowers and incense. The Brahmans come and invite the Buddhas to enter the city. These do so in order, and remain two nights in it. All through the night they keep lamps burning, have skilful music, and present offerings. This is the practice in all the other kingdoms as well. The Heads of the Vaisya families in them establish in the cities houses for dispensing charity and medicines. All the poor and destitute in the country, orphans, widowers, and childless men, maimed people and cripples, and all who are diseased, go to those houses, and are provided with every kind of help, and doctors examine their diseases. They get the food and medicines which their cases require, and are made to feel at ease; and when they are better, they go away of themselves.

When king Asoka destroyed the seven topes, (intending) to make eighty-four thousand,[9] the first which he made was the great tope, more than three le to the south of this city. In front of this there is a footprint of Buddha, where a vihara has been built. The door of it faces the north, and on the south of it there is a stone pillar, fourteen or fifteen cubits in circumference, and more than thirty cubits high, on which there is an inscription, saying, "Asoka gave the jambudvipa to the general body of all the monks, and then redeemed it from them with money. This he did three times."[10] North from the tope 300 or 400 paces, king Asoka built the city of Ne-le.[11] In it there is a stone pillar, which also is more than thirty feet high, with a lion on the top of it. On the pillar there is an inscription recording the things which led to the building of Ne-le, with the number of the year, the day, and the month.

NOTES

[1] The modern Patna, lat. 25d 28s N., lon. 85d 15s E. The Sanskrit name means "The city of flowers." It is the Indian Florence.

[2] See chap. x, note 3. Asoka transferred his court from Rajagriha to Pataliputtra, and there, in the eighteenth year of his reign, he convoked the third Great Synod,--according, at least, to southern Buddhism. It must have

been held a few years before B.C. 250; Eitel says in 246.

[3] "The Vulture-hill;" so called because Mara, according to Buddhist tradition, once assumed the form of a vulture on it to interrupt the meditation of Ananda; or, more probably, because it was a resort of vultures. It was near Rajagriha, the earlier capital of Asoka, so that Fa-hien connects a legend of it with his account of Patna. It abounded in caverns, and was famous as a resort of ascetics.

[4] A Brahman by cast, but a Buddhist in faith.

[5] So, by the help of Julien's "Methode," I transliterate the Chinese characters {.} {.} {.} {.}. Beal gives Radhasvami, his Chinese text having a {.} between {.} and {.}. I suppose the name was Radhasvami or Radhasami.

[6] {.} {.}, the names of two kinds of schools, often occurring in the Li Ki and Mencius. Why should there not have been schools in those monasteries in India as there were in China? Fa-hien himself grew up with other boys in a monastery, and no doubt had to "go to school." And the next sentence shows us there might be schools for more advanced students as well as for the Sramaneras.

[7] See chap. xvi, note 22. It is perhaps with reference to the famous Bodhisattva that the Brahman here is said to be "also" named Manjusri.

[8] ? Cashmere cloth.

[9] See chap. xxiii, note 3.

[10] We wish that we had more particulars of this great transaction, and that we knew what value in money Asoka set on the whole world. It is to be observed that he gave it to the monks, and did not receive it from them. Their right was from him, and he bought it back. He was the only "Power" that was.

[11] We know nothing more of Ne-le. It could only have been a small place;

an outpost for the defence of Pataliputtra.

CHAPTER XXVIII

RAJAGRIHA, NEW AND OLD. LEGENDS AND INCIDENTS CONNECTED WITH IT.

(The travellers) went on from this to the south-east for nine yojanas, and came to a small solitary rocky hill,[1] at the head or end of which[2] was an apartment of stone, facing the south,--the place where Buddha sat, when Sakra, Ruler of Devas, brought the deva-musician, Pancha-(sikha),[3] to give pleasure to him by playing on his lute. Sakra then asked Buddha about forty-two subjects, tracing (the questions) out with his finger one by one on the rock.[4] The prints of his tracing are still there; and here also there is a monastery.

A yojana south-west from this place brought them to the village of Nala,[5] where Sariputtra[6] was born, and to which also he returned, and attained here his pari-nirvana. Over the spot (where his body was burned) there was built a tope, which is still in existence.

Another yojana to the west brought them to New Rajagriha,[7]--the new city which was built by king Ajatasatru. There were two monasteries in it. Three hundred paces outside the west gate, king Ajatasatru, having obtained one portion of the relics of Buddha, built (over them) a tope, high, large, grand, and beautiful. Leaving the city by the south gate, and proceeding south four le, one enters a valley, and comes to a circular space formed by five hills, which stand all round it, and have the appearance of the suburban wall of a city. Here was the old city of king Bimbisara; from east to west about five or six le, and from north to south seven or eight. It was here that Sariputtra and Maudgalyayana first saw Upasena;[8] that the Nirgrantha[9] made a pit of fire and poisoned the rice, and then invited Buddha (to eat with him); that king Ajatasatru made a black elephant intoxicated with liquor, wishing him to injure Buddha;[10] and that at the north-east corner of the city in a (large) curving (space) Jivaka built a vihara in the garden of Ambapali,[11] and invited Buddha with his 1250 disciples to it, that he might there make his offerings to support them. (These places) are still there as of old, but inside the city all is emptiness and desolation; no man dwells in it.

NOTES

[1] Called by Hsuan-chwang Indra-sila-guha, or "The cavern of Indra." It has been identified with a hill near the village of Giryek, on the bank of the Panchana river, about thirty-six miles from Gaya. The hill terminates in two peaks overhanging the river, and it is the more northern and higher of these which Fa-hien had in mind. It bears an oblong terrace covered with the ruins of several buildings, especially of a vihara.

[2] This does not mean the top or summit of the hill, but its "headland," where it ended at the river.

[3] See the account of this visit of Sakra in M. B., pp. 288-290. It is from Hardy that we are able to complete here the name of the musician, which appears in Fa-hien as only Pancha, or "Five." His harp or lute, we are told, was "twelve miles long."

[4] Hardy (M. B., pp. 288, 289) makes the subjects only thirteen, which are still to be found in one of the Sutras ("the Dik-Sanga, in the Sakra-prasna Sutra"). Whether it was Sakra who wrote his questions, or Buddha who wrote the answers, depends on the punctuation. It seems better to make Sakra the writer.

[5] Or Nalanda; identified with the present Baragong. A grand monastery was subsequently built at it, famous by the residence for five years of Hsuan-chwang.

[6] See chap. xvi, note 11. There is some doubt as to the statement that Nala was his birthplace.

[7] The city of "Royal Palaces;" "the residence of the Magadha kings from Bimbisara to Asoka, the first metropolis of Buddhism, at the foot of the

Gridhrakuta mountains. Here the first synod assembled within a year after Sakyamuni's death. Its ruins are still extant at the village of Rajghir, sixteen miles S.W. of Behar, and form an object of pilgrimage to the Jains (E. H., p. 100)." It is called New Rajagriha to distinguish it from Kusagarapura, a few miles from it, the old residence of the kings. Eitel says it was built by Bimbisara, while Fa-hien ascribes it to Ajatasatru. I suppose the son finished what the father had begun.

[8] One of the five first followers of Sakyamuni. He is also called Asvajit; in Pali Assaji; but Asvajit seems to be a military title= "Master or trainer of horses." The two more famous disciples met him, not to lead him, but to be directed by him, to Buddha. See Sacred Books of the East, vol. xiii, Vinaya Texts, pp. 144-147.

[9] One of the six Tirthyas (Tirthakas="erroneous teachers;" M. B., pp. 290-292, but I have not found the particulars of the attempts on Buddha's life referred to by Fa-hien), or Brahmanical opponents of Buddha. He was an ascetic, one of the Jnati clan, and is therefore called Nirgranthajnati. He taught a system of fatalism, condemned the use of clothes, and thought he could subdue all passions by fasting. He had a body of followers, who called themselves by his name (Eitel, pp. 84, 85), and were the forerunners of the Jains.

[10] The king was moved to this by Devadatta. Of course the elephant disappointed them, and did homage to Sakyamuni. See Sacred Books of the East, vol. xx, Vinaya Texts, p. 247.

[11] See chap. xxv, note 3. Jivaka was Ambapali's son by king Bimbisara, and devoted himself to the practice of medicine. See the account of him in the Sacred Books of the East, vol. xvii, Vinaya Texts, pp. 171-194.

CHAPTER XXIX

GRIDHRA-KUTA HILL, AND LEGENDS. FA-HIEN PASSES A NIGHT ON IT. HIS REFLECTIONS.

Entering the valley, and keeping along the mountains on the south- east, after ascending fifteen le, (the travellers) came to mount Gridhra-kuta.[1] Three le before you reach the top, there is a cavern in the rocks, facing the south, in which Buddha sat in meditation. Thirty paces to the north-west there is another, where Ananda was sitting in meditation, when the deva Mara Pisuna,[2] having assumed the form of a large vulture, took his place in front of the cavern, and frightened the disciple. Then Buddha, by his mysterious, supernatural power, made a cleft in the rock, introduced his hand, and stroked Ananda's shoulder, so that his fear immediately passed away. The footprints of the bird and the cleft for (Buddha's) hand are still there, and hence comes the name of "The Hill of the Vulture Cavern."

In front of the cavern there are the places where the four Buddhas sat. There are caverns also of the Arhats, one where each sat and meditated, amounting to several hundred in all. At the place where in front of his rocky apartment Buddha was walking from east to west (in meditation), and Devadatta, from among the beetling cliffs on the north of the mountain, threw a rock across, and hurt Buddha's toes,[3] the rock is still there.[4]

The hall where Buddha preached his Law has been destroyed, and only the foundations of the brick walls remain. On this hill the peak is beautifully green, and rises grandly up; it is the highest of all the five hills. In the New City Fa-hien bought incense-(sticks), flowers, oil and lamps, and hired two bhikshus, long resident (at the place), to carry them (to the peak). When he himself got to it, he made his offerings with the flowers and incense, and lighted the lamps when the darkness began to come on. He felt melancholy, but restrained his tears and said, "Here Buddha delivered the Surangama (Sutra).[5] I, Fa-hien, was born when I could not meet with Buddha; and now I only see the footprints which he has left, and the place where he lived, and nothing more." With this, in front of the rock cavern, he chanted the Surangama Sutra, remained there over the night, and then returned towards the New City.[6]

NOTES

[1] See chap. xxviii, note 1.

[2] See chap. xxv, note 9. Pisuna is a name given to Mara, and signifies "sinful lust."

[3] See M. B., p. 320. Hardy says that Devadatta's attempt was "by the help of a machine;" but the oldest account in the Sacred Books of the East, vol. xx, Vinaya Texts, p. 245, agrees with what Fa-hien implies that he threw the rock with his own arm.

[4] And, as described by Hsuan-chwang, fourteen or fifteen cubits high, and thirty paces round.

[5] See Mr. Bunyiu Nanjio's "Catalogue of the Chinese Translation of the Buddhist Tripitaka," Sutra Pitaka, Nos. 399, 446. It was the former of these that came on this occasion to the thoughts and memory of Fa-hien.

[6] In a note (p. lx) to his revised version of our author, Mr. Beal says, "There is a full account of this perilous visit of Fa-hien, and how he was attacked by tigers, in the 'History of the High Priests.'" But "the high priests" merely means distinguished monks, "eminent monks," as Mr. Nanjio exactly renders the adjectival character. Nor was Fa-hien "attacked by tigers" on the peak. No "tigers" appear in the Memoir. "Two black lions" indeed crouched before him for a time this night, "licking their lips and waving their tails;" but their appearance was to "try," and not to attack him; and when they saw him resolute, they "drooped their heads, put down their tails, and prostrated themselves before him." This of course is not an historical account, but a legendary tribute to his bold perseverance.

CHAPTER XXX

THE SRATAPARNA CAVE, OR CAVE OF THE FIRST COUNCIL. LEGENDS. SUICIDE OF A BHIKSHU.

Out from the old city, after walking over 300 paces, on the west of the road, (the travellers) found the Karanda Bamboo garden,[1] where the (old) vihara is still in existence, with a company of monks, who keep (the ground about it) swept and watered.

North of the vihara two or three le there was the Smasanam, which name means in Chinese "the field of graves into which the dead are thrown."[2]

As they kept along the mountain on the south, and went west for 300 paces, they found a dwelling among the rocks, named the Pippala cave,[3] in which Buddha regularly sat in meditation after taking his (midday) meal.

Going on still to the west for five or six le, on the north of the hill, in the shade, they found the cavern called Srataparna,[4] the place where, after the nirvana[5] of Buddha, 500 Arhats collected the Sutras. When they brought the Sutras forth, three lofty seats[6] had been prepared and grandly ornamented. Sariputtra occupied the one on the left, and Maudgalyayana that on the right. Of the number of five hundred one was wanting. Mahakasyapa was president (on the middle seat). Amanda was then outside the door, and could not get in.[7] At the place there was (subsequently) raised a tope, which is still existing.

Along (the sides of) the hill, there are also a very great many cells among the rocks, where the various Arhans sat and meditated. As you leave the old city on the north, and go down east for three le, there is the rock dwelling of Devadatta, and at a distance of fifty paces from it there is a large, square, black rock. Formerly there was a bhikshu, who, as he walked backwards and forwards upon it, thought with himself:--"This body[8] is impermanent, a thing of bitterness and vanity,[9] and which cannot be looked on as pure.[10] I am weary of this body, and troubled by it as an evil." With this he grasped a knife, and was about to kill himself. But he thought again:--"The World-honoured one laid down a prohibition against one's killing himself."[11] Further it occurred to him:--"Yes, he did; but I now only wish to kill three poisonous thieves."[12] Immediately with the knife he cut his throat. With the first gash into the flesh he attained the state of a Srotapanna;[13] when he had gone half through, he attained to be an Anagamin;[14] and when he had cut right through, he was an Arhat, and attained to pari-nirvana;[15] (and died).

NOTES

[1] Karanda Venuvana; a park presented to Buddha by king Bimbisara, who also built a vihara in it. See the account of the transaction in M. B., p. 194. The place was called Karanda, from a creature so named, which awoke the king just as a snake was about to bite him, and thus saved his life. In Hardy the creature appears as a squirrel, but Eitel says that the Karanda is a bird of sweet voice, resembling a magpie, but herding in flocks; the /cuculus melanoleucus/. See "Buddhist Birth Stories," p. 118.

[2] The language here is rather contemptuous, as if our author had no sympathy with any other mode of disposing of the dead, but by his own Buddhistic method of cremation.

[3] The Chinese characters used for the name of this cavern serve also to name the pippala (peepul) tree, the /ficus religiosa/. They make us think that there was such a tree overshadowing the cave; but Fa-hien would hardly have neglected to mention such a circumstance.

[4] A very great place in the annals of Buddhism. The Council in the Srataparna cave did not come together fortuitously, but appears to have been convoked by the older members to settle the rules and doctrines of the order. The cave was prepared for the occasion by king Ajatasatru. From the expression about the "bringing forth of the King," it would seem that the Sutras or some of them had been already committed to writing. May not the meaning of King {.} here be extended to the Vinaya rules, as well as the Sutras, and mean "the standards" of the system generally? See Davids' Manual, chapter ix, and Sacred Books of the East, vol. xx, Vinaya Texts, pp. 370-385.

[5] So in the text, evidently for pari-nirvana.

[6] Instead of "high" seats, the Chinese texts have "vacant." The character for "prepared" denotes "spread;"--they were carpeted; perhaps, both cushioned and carpeted, being rugs spread on the ground, raised higher than the other places for seats.

[7] Did they not contrive to let him in, with some cachinnation, even in so august an assembly, that so important a member should have been shut out?

[8] "The life of this body" would, I think, fairly express the idea of the bhikshu.

[9] See the account of Buddha's preaching in chapter xviii.

[10] The sentiment of this clause is not easily caught.

[11] See E. M., p. 152:--"Buddha made a law forbidding the monks to commit suicide. He prohibited any one from discoursing on the miseries of life in such a manner as to cause desperation." See also M. B., pp. 464, 465.

[12] Beal says:--"Evil desire; hatred; ignorance."

[13] See chap. xx, note 10.

[14] The Anagamin belong to the third degree of Buddhistic saintship, the third class of Aryas, who are no more liable to be reborn as men, but are to be born once more as devas, when they will forthwith become Arhats, and attain to nirvana. E. H., pp. 8, 9.

[15] Our author expresses no opinion of his own on the act of this bhikshu. Must it not have been a good act, when it was attended, in the very act of performance, by such blessed consequences? But if Buddhism had not something better to show than what appears here, it would not attract the interest which it now does. The bhikshu was evidently rather out of his mind; and the verdict of a coroner's inquest of this nineteenth century would have pronounced that he killed himself "in a fit of insanity."

CHAPTER XXXI

GAYA. SAKYAMUNI'S ATTAINING TO THE BUDDHASHIP; AND OTHER LEGENDS.

From this place, after travelling to the west for four yojanas, (the pilgrims) came to the city of Gaya;[1] but inside the city all was emptiness and desolation. Going on again to the south for twenty le, they arrived at the place where the Bodhisattva for six years practised with himself painful austerities. All around was forest.

Three le west from here they came to the place where, when Buddha had gone into the water to bathe, a deva bent down the branch of a tree, by means of which he succeeded in getting out of the pool.[2]

Two le north from this was the place where the Gramika girls presented to Buddha the rice-gruel made with milk;[3] and two le north from this (again) was the place where, seated on a rock under a great tree, and facing the east, he ate (the gruel). The tree and the rock are there at the present day. The rock may be six cubits in breadth and length, and rather more than two cubits in height. In Central India the cold and heat are so equally tempered that trees will live in it for several thousand and even for ten thousand years.

Half a yojana from this place to the north-east there was a cavern in the rocks, into which the Bodhisattva entered, and sat cross-legged with his face to the west. (As he did so), he said to himself, "If I am to attain to perfect wisdom (and become Buddha), let there be a supernatural attestation of it." On the wall of the rock there appeared immediately the shadow of a Buddha, rather more than three feet in length, which is still bright at the present day. At this moment heaven and earth were greatly moved, and devas in the air spoke plainly, "This is not the place where any Buddha of the past, or he that is to come, has attained, or will attain, to perfect Wisdom. Less than half a yojana from this to the south-west will bring you to the patra[4] tree, where all past Buddhas have attained, and all to come must attain, to perfect Wisdom." When they had spoken these words, they immediately led the way forwards to the place, singing as they did so. As they thus went away, the Bodhisattva arose and walked (after them). At a distance of thirty paces from the tree, a deva gave him the grass of lucky omen,[5] which he received and went on. After (he had proceeded) fifteen paces, 500 green birds came flying towards him, went round him thrice, and disappeared. The Bodhisattva went

106

forward to the patra tree, placed the kusa grass at the foot of it, and sat down with his face to the east. Then king Mara sent three beautiful young ladies, who came from the north, to tempt him, while he himself came from the south to do the same. The Bodhisattva put his toes down on the ground, and the demon soldiers retired and dispersed, and the three young ladies were changed into old (grand-)mothers.[6]

At the place mentioned above of the six years' painful austerities, and at all these other places, men subsequently reared topes and set up images, which all exist at the present day.

Where Buddha, after attaining to perfect wisdom, for seven days contemplated the tree, and experienced the joy of vimukti;[7] where, under the patra tree, he walked backwards and forwards from west to east for seven days; where the devas made a hall appear, composed of the seven precious substances, and presented offerings to him for seven days; where the blind dragon Muchilinda[8] encircled him for seven days; where he sat under the nyagrodha tree, on a square rock, with his face to the east, and Brahma-deva[9] came and made his request to him; where the four deva kings brought to him their alms- bowls;[10] where the 500 merchants[11] presented to him the roasted flour and honey; and where he converted the brothers Kasyapa and their thousand disciples;[12]--at all these places topes were reared.

At the place where Buddha attained to perfect Wisdom, there are three monasteries, in all of which there are monks residing. The families of their people around supply the societies of these monks with an abundant sufficiency of what they require, so that there is no lack or stint.[13] The disciplinary rules are strictly observed by them. The laws regulating their demeanour in sitting, rising, and entering when the others are assembled, are those which have been practised by all the saints since Buddha was in the world down to the present day. The places of the four great topes have been fixed, and handed down without break, since Buddha attained to nirvana. Those four great topes are those at the places where Buddha was born; where he attained to Wisdom; where he (began to) move the wheel of his Law; and where he attained to pari-nirvana.

NOTES

[1] Gaya, a city of Magadha, was north-west of the present Gayah (lat. 24d 47s N., lon. 85d 1s E). It was here that Sakyamuni lived for seven years, after quitting his family, until he attained to Buddhaship. The place is still frequented by pilgrims. E. H., p. 41.

[2] This is told so as to make us think that he was in danger of being drowned; but this does not appear in the only other account of the incident I have met with,--in "The Life of the Buddha," p. 31. And he was not yet Buddha, though he is here called so; unless indeed the narrative is confused, and the incidents do not follow in the order of time.

[3] An incident similar to this is told, with many additions, in Hardy's M. B., pp. 166-168; "The Life of the Buddha," p. 30; and the "Buddhist Birth Stories," pp. 91, 92; but the name of the ministering girl or girls is different. I take Gramika from a note in Beal's revised version; it seems to me a happy solution of the difficulty caused by the {.} {.} of Fa-hien.

[4] Called "the tree of leaves," and "the tree of reflection;" a palm tree, the /borassus flabellifera/, described as a tree which never loses its leaves. It is often confounded with the pippala. E. H., p. 92.

[5] The kusa grass, mentioned in a previous note.

[6] See the account of this contest with Mara in M. B., pp. 171-179, and "Buddhist Birth Stories," pp. 96-101.

[7] See chap. xiii, note 7.

[8] Called also Maha, or the Great Muchilinda. Eitel says: "A naga king, the tutelary deity of a lake near which Sakyamuni once sat for seven days absorbed in meditation, whilst the king guarded him." The account (p. 35) in "The Life of the Buddha" is:--"Buddha went to where lived the naga king Muchilinda, and he, wishing to preserve him from the sun and rain, wrapped

his body seven times round him, and spread out his hood over his head; and there he remained seven days in thought." So also the Nidana Katha, in "Buddhist Birth Stories," p. 109.

[9] This was Brahma himself, though "king" is omitted. What he requested of the Buddha was that he would begin the preaching of his Law. Nidana Katha, p. 111.

[10] See chap. xii, note 10.

[11] The other accounts mention only two; but in M. B., p. 182, and the Nidana Katha, p. 110, these two have 500 well-laden waggons with them.

[12] These must not be confounded with Mahakasyapa of chap. xvi, note 17. They were three brothers, Uruvilva, Gaya, and Nadi-Kasyapa, up to this time holders of "erroneous" views, having 500, 300, and 200 disciples respectively. They became distinguished followers of Sakyamuni; and are--each of them--to become Buddha by-and-by. See the Nidana Katha, pp. 114, 115.

[13] This seems to be the meaning; but I do not wonder that some understand the sentence of the benevolence of the monkish population to the travellers.

CHAPTER XXXII

LEGEND OF KING ASOKA IN A FORMER BIRTH, AND HIS NARAKA.

When king Asoka, in a former birth,[1] was a little boy and played on the road, he met Kasyapa Buddha walking. (The stranger) begged food, and the boy pleasantly took a handful of earth and gave it to him. The Buddha took the earth, and returned it to the ground on which he was walking; but because of this (the boy) received the recompense of becoming a king of the iron wheel,[2] to rule over Jambudvipa. (Once) when he was making a judicial tour of inspection through Jambudvipa, he saw, between the iron circuit of the two hills, a naraka[3] for the punishment of wicked men. Having thereupon asked his ministers what sort of a thing it was, they replied, "It belongs to Yama,[4] king of demons, for punishing wicked people." The king thought within himself: --"(Even) the king of demons is able to make a naraka in which to deal with wicked men; why should not I, who am the lord of men, make a naraka in which to deal with wicked men?" He forthwith asked his ministers who could make for him a naraka and preside over the punishment of wicked people in it. They replied that it was only a man of extreme wickedness who could make it; and the king thereupon sent officers to seek everywhere for (such) a bad man; and they saw by the side of a pond a man tall and strong, with a black countenance, yellow hair, and green eyes, hooking up the fish with his feet, while he called to him birds and beasts, and, when they came, then shot and killed them, so that not one escaped. Having got this man, they took him to the king, who secretly charged him, "You must make a square enclosure with high walls. Plant in it all kinds of flowers and fruits; make good ponds in it for bathing; make it grand and imposing in every way, so that men shall look to it with thirsting desire; make its gates strong and sure; and when any one enters, instantly seize him and punish him as a sinner, not allowing him to get out. Even if I should enter, punish me as a sinner in the same way, and do not let me go. I now appoint you master of that naraka."

Soon after this a bhikshu, pursuing his regular course of begging his food, entered the gate (of the place). When the lictors of the naraka saw him, they were about to subject him to their tortures; but he, frightened, begged them to allow him a moment in which to eat his midday meal. Immediately after, there came in another man, whom they thrust into a mortar and pounded till a red froth overflowed. As the bhikshu looked on, there came to him the thought of the impermanence, the painful suffering and insanity of this body, and how it is but as a bubble and as foam; and instantly he attained to Arhatship. Immediately after, the lictors seized him, and threw him into a caldron of boiling water. There was a look of joyful satisfaction, however, in the bhikshu's countenance. The fire was extinguished, and the water became cold. In the middle (of the caldron) there rose up a lotus flower, with the bhikshu seated on it. The lictors at once went and reported to the king that there was a marvellous occurrence in the naraka, and wished him to go and see it; but the king said, "I formerly made such an agreement that now I dare not go (to the place)." The lictors said, "This is not a small matter. Your majesty ought to go quickly. Let your former agreement be altered." The king thereupon followed them, and entered (the naraka), when the bhikshu preached the Law to him, and he believed, and was made free.[5] Forthwith he demolished the naraka, and repented of all the evil which he had formerly done. From this time he believed in and honoured the Three Precious Ones, and constantly went to a patra tree, repenting under it, with self-reproach, of his errors, and accepting the eight rules of abstinence.[6]

The queen asked where the king was constantly going to, and the ministers replied that he was constantly to be seen under (such and such) a patra tree. She watched for a time when the king was not there, and then sent men to cut the tree down. When the king came, and saw what had been done, he swooned away with sorrow, and fell to the ground. His ministers sprinkled water on his face, and after a considerable time he revived. He then built all round (the stump) with bricks, and poured a hundred pitchers of cows' milk on the roots; and as he lay with his four limbs spread out on the ground, he took this oath, "If the tree do not live, I will never rise from this." When he had uttered this oath, the tree immediately began to grow from the roots, and it has continued to grow till now, when it is nearly 100 cubits in height.

NOTES

[1] Here is an instance of {.} used, as was pointed out in chap. ix, note 3, for a former age; and not merely a former time. Perhaps "a former birth" is the best translation. The Corean reading of Kasyapa Buddha is certainly preferable to the Chinese "Sakya Buddha."

[2] See chap. xvii, note 8.

[3] I prefer to retain the Sanskrit term here, instead of translating the Chinese text by "Earth's prison {.} {.}," or "a prison in the earth;" the name for which has been adopted generally by Christian missionaries in China for gehenna and hell.

[4] Eitel (p. 173) says:--"Yama was originally the Aryan god of the dead, living in a heaven above the world, the regent of the south; but Brahmanism transferred his abode to hell. Both views have been retained by Buddhism." The Yama of the text is the "regent of the narakas, residing south of Jambudvipa, outside the Chakravalas (the double circuit of mountains above), in a palace built of brass and iron. He has a sister who controls all the female culprits, as he exclusively deals with the male sex. Three times, however, in every twenty-four hours, a demon pours boiling copper into Yama's mouth, and squeezes it down his throat, causing him unspeakable pain." Such, however, is the wonderful "transrotation of births," that when Yama's sins have been expiated, he is to be reborn as Buddha, under the name of "The Universal King."

[5] Or, "was loosed;" from the bonds, I suppose, of his various illusions.

[6] I have not met with this particular numerical category.

CHAPTER XXXIII

MOUNT GURUPADA, WHERE KASYAPA BUDDHA'S ENTIRE SKELETON IS.

(The travellers), going on from this three le to the south, came to a mountain named Gurupada,[1] inside which Mahakasyapa even now is. He made a cleft, and went down into it, though the place where he entered would not (now) admit a man. Having gone down very far, there was a hole on one side, and there the complete body of Kasyapa (still) abides. Outside the hole (at which he entered) is the earth with which he had washed his hands.[2] If the people living thereabouts have a sore on their heads, they plaster on it some of the earth from this, and feel immediately easier.[3] On this mountain, now as of old, there are Arhats abiding. Devotees of our Law from the various countries in that quarter go year by year to the mountain, and present offerings to Kasyapa; and to those whose hearts are strong in faith there come Arhats at night, and talk with them, discussing and explaining their doubts, and disappearing suddenly afterwards.

On this hill hazels grow luxuriously; and there are many lions, tigers, and wolves, so that people should not travel incautiously.

NOTES

[1] "Fowl's-foot hill," "with three peaks, resembling the foot of a chicken. It lies seven miles south-east of Gaya, and was the residence of Mahakasyapa, who is said to be still living inside this mountain." So Eitel says, p. 58; but this chapter does not say that Kasyapa is in the mountain alive, but that his body entire is in a recess or hole in it. Hardy (M. B., p. 97) says that after Kasyapa Buddha's body was burnt, the bones still remained in their usual position, presenting the appearance of a perfect skeleton. It is of him that the chapter speaks, and not of the famous disciple of Sakyamuni, who also is called Mahakasyapa. This will appear also on a comparison of Eitel's articles on "Mahakasyapa" and "Kasyapa Buddha."

[2] Was it a custom to wash the hands with "earth," as is often done with sand?

[3] This I conceive to be the meaning here.

CHAPTER XXXIV

ON THE WAY BACK TO PATNA. VARANASI, OR BENARES. SAKYAMUNI'S FIRST DOINGS AFTER BECOMING BUDDHA.

Fa-hien[1] returned (from here) towards Pataliputtra,[2] keeping along the course of the Ganges and descending in the direction of the west. After going ten yojanas he found a vihara, named "The Wilderness,"--a place where Buddha had dwelt, and where there are monks now.

Pursuing the same course, and going still to the west, he arrived, after twelve yojanas, at the city of Varanasi[3] in the kingdom of Kasi. Rather more than ten le to the north-east of the city, he found the vihara in the park of "The rishi's Deer-wild."[4] In this park there formerly resided a Pratyeka Buddha,[5] with whom the deer were regularly in the habit of stopping for the night. When the World-honoured one was about to attain to perfect Wisdom, the devas sang in the sky, "The son of king Suddhodana, having quitted his family and studied the Path (of Wisdom),[6] will now in seven days become Buddha." The Pratyeka Buddha heard their words, and immediately attained to nirvana; and hence this place was named "The Park of the rishi's Deer-wild."[7] After the World-honoured one had attained to perfect Wisdom, men build the vihara in it.

Buddha wished to convert Kaundinya[8] and his four companions; but they, (being aware of his intention), said to one another, "This Sramana Gotama[9] for six years continued in the practice of painful austerities, eating daily (only) a single hemp-seed, and one grain of rice, without attaining to the Path (of Wisdom); how much less will he do so now that he has entered (again) among men, and is giving the reins to (the indulgence of) his body, his speech, and his thoughts! What has he to do with the Path (of Wisdom)? To-day, when he comes to us, let us be on our guard not to speak with him." At the places where the five men all rose up, and respectfully saluted (Buddha), when he came to them; where, sixty paces north from this, he sat with his face to the east, and first turned the wheel of the Law, converting Kaundinya and the four others; where, twenty paces further to the north, he delivered his prophecy concerning Maitreya;[10] and where, at a distance of fifty paces to the south, the dragon Elapattra[11] asked him, "When shall I get free from this naga body?"--at all these places topes were reared, and are still existing. In (the park) there are two monasteries, in both of which there are monks residing.

When you go north-west from the vihara of the Deer-wild park for thirteen yojanas, there is a kingdom named Kausambi.[12] Its vihara is named Ghochiravana[13]--a place where Buddha formerly resided. Now, as of old, there is a company of monks there, most of whom are students of the hinayana.

East from (this), when you have travelled eight yojanas, is the place where Buddha converted[14] the evil demon. There, and where he walked (in meditation) and sat at the place which was his regular abode, there have been topes erected. There is also a monastery, which may contain more than

114

a hundred monks.

NOTES

[1] Fa-hien is here mentioned singly, as in the account of his visit to the cave on Gridhra-kuta. I think that Tao-ching may have remained at Patna after their first visit to it.

[2] See chap. xxvii, note 1.

[3] "The city surrounded by rivers;" the modern Benares, lat. 25d 23s N., lon. 83d 5s E.

[4] "The rishi," says Eitel, "is a man whose bodily frame has undergone a certain transformation by dint of meditation and asceticism, so that he is, for an indefinite period, exempt from decrepitude, age, and death. As this period is believed to extend far beyond the usual duration of human life, such persons are called, and popularly believed to be, immortals." Rishis are divided into various classes; and rishi-ism is spoken of as a seventh part of transrotation, and rishis are referred to as the seventh class of sentient beings. Taoism, as well as Buddhism, has its Seen jin.

[5] See chap. xiii, note 15.

[6] See chap. xxii, note 2.

[7] For another legend about this park, and the identification of "a fine wood" still existing, see note in Beal's first version, p. 135.

[8] A prince of Magadha and a maternal uncle of Sakyamuni, who gave him the name of Ajnata, meaning automat; and hence he often appears as Ajnata Kaundinya. He and his four friends had followed Sakyamuni into the Uruvilva desert, sympathising with him in the austerities he endured, and hoping that they would issue in his Buddhaship. They were not aware that that issue had come; which may show us that all the accounts in the thirty-first chapter are merely descriptions, by means of external imagery, of

115

what had taken place internally. The kingdom of nirvana had come without observation. These friends knew it not; and they were offended by what they considered Sakyamuni's failure, and the course he was now pursuing. See the account of their conversion in M. B., p. 186.

[9] This is the only instance in Fa-hien's text where the Bodhisattva or Buddha is called by the surname "Gotama." For the most part our traveller uses Buddha as a proper name, though it properly means "The Enlightened." He uses also the combinations "Sakya Buddha,"="The Buddha of the Sakya tribe," and "Sakyamuni,"="The Sakya sage." This last is the most common designation of the Buddha in China, and to my mind best combines the characteristics of a descriptive and a proper name. Among other Buddhistic peoples "Gotama" and "Gotama Buddha" are the more frequent designations. It is not easy to account for the rise of the surname Gotama in the Sakya family, as Oldenberg acknowledges. He says that "the Sakyas, in accordance with the custom of Indian noble families, had borrowed it from one of the ancient Vedic bard families." Dr. Davids ("Buddhism," p. 27) says: "The family name was certainly Gautama," adding in a note, "It is a curious fact that Gautama is still the family name of the Rajput chiefs of Nagara, the village which has been identified with Kapilavastu." Dr. Eitel says that "Gautama was the sacerdotal name of the Sakya family, which counted the ancient rishi Gautama among its ancestors." When we proceed, however, to endeavour to trace the connexion of that Brahmanical rishi with the Sakya house, by means of 1323, 1468, 1469, and other historical works in Nanjio's Catalogue, we soon find that Indian histories have no surer foundation than the shifting sand;--see E. H., on the name Sakya, pp. 108, 109. We must be content for the present simply to accept Gotama as one of the surnames of the Buddha with whom we have to do.

[10] See chap. vi, note 5. It is there said that the prediction of Maitreya's succession to the Buddhaship was made to him in the Tushita heaven. Was there a repetition of it here in the Deer-park, or was a prediction now given concerning something else?

[11] Nothing seems to be known of this naga but what we read here.

[12] Identified by some with Kusia, near Kurrah (lat. 25d 41s N., lon. 81d 27s E.); by others with Kosam on the Jumna, thirty miles above Allahabad. See E. H., p. 55.

[13] Ghochira was the name of a Vaisya elder, or head, who presented a garden and vihara to Buddha. Hardy (M. B., p. 356) quotes a statement from a Singhalese authority that Sakyamuni resided here during the ninth year of his Buddhaship.

[14] Dr. Davids thinks this may refer to the striking and beautiful story of the conversion of the Yakkha Alavaka, as related in the Uragavagga, Alavakasutta, pp. 29-31 (Sacred Books of the East, vol. x, part ii).

CHAPTER XXXV

DAKSHINA, AND THE PIGEON MONASTERY.

South from this 200 yojanas, there is a country named Dakshina,[1] where there is a monastery (dedicated to) the bygone Kasyapa Buddha, and which has been hewn out from a large hill of rock. It consists in all of five storeys;--the lowest, having the form of an elephant, with 500 apartments in the rock; the second, having the form of a lion, with 400 apartments; the third, having the form of a horse, with 300 apartments; the fourth, having the form of an ox, with 200 apartments; and the fifth, having the form of a pigeon, with 100 apartments. At the very top there is a spring, the water of which, always in front of the apartments in the rock, goes round among the rooms, now circling, now curving, till in this way it arrives at the lowest storey, having followed the shape of the structure, and flows out there at the door. Everywhere in the apartments of the monks, the rock has been pierced so as to form windows for the admission of light, so that they are all bright, without any being left in darkness. At the four corners of the (tiers of) apartments, the rock has been hewn so as to form steps for ascending to the top (of each). The men of the present day, being of small size, and going up step by step, manage to get to the top; but in a former age, they did so at one step.[2] Because of this, the monastery is called Paravata, that being the Indian name for a pigeon. There are always Arhats residing in it.

The country about is (a tract of) uncultivated hillocks,[3] without inhabitants. At a very long distance from the hill there are villages, where the people all have bad and erroneous views, and do not know the Sramanas of the Law of Buddha, Brahmanas, or (devotees of) any of the other and different schools. The people of that country are constantly seeing men on the wing, who come and enter this monastery. On one occasion, when devotees of various countries came to perform their worship at it, the people of those villages said to them, "Why do you not fly? The devotees whom we have seen hereabouts all fly;" and the strangers answered, on the spur of the moment, "Our wings are not yet fully formed."

The kingdom of Dakshina is out of the way, and perilous to traverse. There are difficulties in connexion with the roads; but those who know how to manage such difficulties and wish to proceed should bring with them money and various articles, and give them to the king. He will then send men to escort them. These will (at different stages) pass them over to others, who will show them the shortest routes. Fa-hien, however, was after all unable to go there; but having received the (above) accounts from men of the country, he has narrated them.

NOTES

[1] Said to be the ancient name of the Deccan. As to the various marvels in the chapter, it must be borne in mind that our author, as he tells us at the end, only gives them from hearsay. See "Buddhist Records of the Western World," vol. ii, pp. 214, 215, where the description, however, is very different.

[2] Compare the account of Buddha's great stride of fifteen yojanas in Ceylon, as related in chapter xxxviii.

[3] See the same phrase in the Books of the Later Han dynasty, the twenty-fourth Book of Biographies, p. 9b.

CHAPTER XXXVI

IN PATNA. FA-HIEN'S LABOURS IN TRANSCRIPTION OF
MANUSCRIPTS, AND INDIAN STUDIES FOR THREE YEARS.

From Varanasi (the travellers) went back east to Pataliputtra. Fa-hien's original object had been to search for (copies of) the Vinaya. In the various kingdoms of North India, however, he had found one master transmitting orally (the rules) to another, but no written copies which he could transcribe. He had therefore travelled far and come on to Central India. Here, in the mahayana monastery,[1] he found a copy of the Vinaya, containing the Mahasanghika[2] rules,--those which were observed in the first Great Council, while Buddha was still in the world. The original copy was handed down in the Jetavana vihara. As to the other eighteen schools,[3] each one has the views and decisions of its own masters. Those agree (with this) in the general meaning, but they have small and trivial differences, as when one opens and another shuts.[4] This copy (of the rules), however, is the most complete, with the fullest explanations.[5]

He further got a transcript of the rules in six or seven thousand gathas,[6] being the sarvastivadah[7] rules,--those which are observed by the communities of monks in the land of Ts'in; which also have all been handed down orally from master to master without being committed to writing. In the community here, moreover, we got the Samyuktabhi-dharma-hridaya-(sastra),[8] containing about six or seven thousand gathas; he also got a Sutra of 2500 gathas; one chapter of the Parinir-vana-vaipulya Sutra,[9] of about 5000 gathas; and the Mahasan- ghikah Abhidharma.

In consequence (of this success in his quest) Fa-hien stayed here for three years, learning Sanskrit books and the Sanskrit speech, and writing out the Vinaya rules. When Tao-ching arrived in the Central Kingdom, and saw the rules observed by the Sramanas, and the dignified demeanour in their societies which he remarked under all occurring circumstances, he sadly called to mind in what a mutilated and imperfect condition the rules were among the monkish communities in the land of Ts'in, and made the following aspiration:--"From this time forth till I come to the state of Buddha, let me not be born in a frontier land."[10] He remained accordingly (in India), and did not return (to the land of Han). Fa-hien, however, whose original purpose had been to secure the introduction of the complete Vinaya rules into the land of Han, returned there alone.

NOTES

[1] Mentioned before in chapter xxvii.

[2] Mahasanghikah simply means "the Great Assembly," that is, of monks. When was this first assembly in the time of Sakyamuni held? It does not appear that the rules observed at it were written down at the time. The document found by Fa-hien would be a record of those rules; or rather a copy of that record. We must suppose that the original record had disappeared from the Jetavana vihara, or Fa-hien would probably have spoken of it when he was there, and copied it, if he had been allowed to do so.

[3] The eighteen pu {.}. Four times in this chapter the character called pu occurs, and in the first and two last instances it can only have the meaning, often belonging to it, of "copy." The second instance, however, is different. How should there be eighteen copies, all different from the original, and from one another, in minor matters? We are compelled to translate--"the eighteen schools," an expression well known in all Buddhist writings. See Rhys Davids' Manual, p. 218, and the authorities there quoted.

[4] This is equivalent to the "binding" and "loosing," "opening" and "shutting," which found their way into the New Testament, and the Christian Church, from the schools of the Jewish Rabbins.

[5] It was afterwards translated by Fa-hien into Chinese. See Nanjio's Catalogue of the Chinese Tripitaka, columns 400 and 401, and Nos. 1119 and 1150, columns 247 and 253.

[6] A gatha is a stanza, generally consisting, it has seemed to me, of a few, commonly of two, lines somewhat metrically arranged; but I do not know that its length is strictly defined.

[7] "A branch," says Eitel, "of the great vaibhashika school, asserting the reality of all visible phenomena, and claiming the authority of Rahula."

[8] See Nanjio's Catalogue, No. 1287. He does not mention it in his account of Fa-hien, who, he says, translated the Samyukta-pitaka Sutra.

[9] Probably Nanjio's Catalogue, No. 120; at any rate, connected with it.

[10] This then would be the consummation of the Sramana's being,--to get to be Buddha, the Buddha of his time in his Kalpa; and Tao-ching thought that he could attain to this consummation by a succession of births; and was likely to attain to it sooner by living only in India. If all this was not in his mind, he yet felt that each of his successive lives would be happier, if lived in India.

CHAPTER XXXVII

TO CHAMPA AND TAMALIPTI. STAY AND LABOURS THERE FOR THREE YEARS. TAKES SHIP TO SINGHALA, OR CEYLON.

Following the course of the Ganges, and descending eastwards for eighteen yojanas, he found on the southern bank the great kingdom of Champa,[1] with topes reared at the places where Buddha walked in meditation by his vihara, and where he and the three Buddhas, his predecessors, sat. There were monks residing at them all. Continuing his journey east for nearly fifty yojanas, he came to the country of Tamalipti,[2] (the capital of which is) a seaport. In the country there are twenty-two monasteries, at all of which there are monks residing. The Law of Buddha is also flourishing in it. Here Fa-hien stayed two years, writing out his Sutras,[3] and drawing pictures of images.

After this he embarked in a large merchant-vessel, and went floating over the sea to the south-west. It was the beginning of winter, and the wind was favourable; and, after fourteen days, sailing day and night, they came to the country of Singhala.[4] The people said that it was distant (from Tamalipti) about 700 yojanas.

The kingdom is on a large island, extending from east to west fifty yojanas, and from north to south thirty. Left and right from it there are as many as 100 small islands, distant from one another ten, twenty, or even 200 le; but all subject to the large island. Most of them produce pearls and precious stones of various kinds; there is one which produces the pure and brilliant pearl,[5]--an island which would form a square of about ten le. The king employs men to watch and protect it, and requires three out of every ten such pearls, which the collectors find.

NOTES

[1] Probably the modern Champanagur, three miles west of Baglipoor, lat. 25d 14s N., lon. 56d 55s E.

[2] Then the principal emporium for the trade with Ceylon and China; the modern Tam-look, lat. 22d 17s N., lon. 88d 2s E.; near the mouth of the Hoogly.

[3] Perhaps Ching {.} is used here for any portions of the Tripitaka which he had obtained.

[4] "The Kingdom of the Lion," Ceylon. Singhala was the name of a merchant adventurer from India, to whom the founding of the kingdom was ascribed. His father was named Singha, "the Lion," which became the name of the country;--Singhala, or Singha-Kingdom, "the Country of the Lion."

[5] Called the mani pearl or bead. Mani is explained as meaning "free from stain," "bright and growing purer." It is a symbol of Buddha and of his Law. The most valuable rosaries are made of manis.

CHAPTER XXXVIII

AT CEYLON. RISE OF THE KINGDOM. FEATS OF BUDDHA. TOPES AND MONASTERIES. STATUE OF BUDDHA IN JADE. BO TREE.

FESTIVAL OF BUDDHA'S TOOTH.

The country originally had no human inhabitants,[1] but was occupied only by spirits and nagas, with which merchants of various countries carried on a trade. When the trafficking was taking place, the spirits did not show themselves. They simply set forth their precious commodities, with labels of the price attached to them; while the merchants made their purchases according to the price; and took the things away.

Through the coming and going of the merchants (in this way), when they went away, the people of (their) various countries heard how pleasant the land was, and flocked to it in numbers till it became a great nation. The (climate) is temperate and attractive, without any difference of summer and winter. The vegetation is always luxuriant. Cultivation proceeds whenever men think fit: there are no fixed seasons for it.

When Buddha came to this country,[2] wishing to transform the wicked nagas, by his supernatural power he planted one foot at the north of the royal city, and the other on the top of a mountain,[3] the two being fifteen yojanas apart. Over the footprint at the north of the city the king built a large tope, 400 cubits high, grandly adorned with gold and silver, and finished with a combination of all the precious substances. By the side of the top he further built a monastery, called the Abhayagiri,[4] where there are (now) five thousand monks. There is in it a hall of Buddha, adorned with carved and inlaid works of gold and silver, and rich in the seven precious substances, in which there is an image (of Buddha) in green jade, more than twenty cubits in height, glittering all over with those substances, and having an appearance of solemn dignity which words cannot express. In the palm of the right hand there is a priceless pearl. Several years had now elapsed since Fa-hien left the land of Han; the men with whom he had been in intercourse had all been of regions strange to him; his eyes had not rested on an old and familiar hill or river, plant or tree; his fellow-travellers, moreover, had been separated from him, some by death, and others flowing off in different directions; no face or shadow was now with him but his own, and a constant sadness was in his heart. Suddenly (one day), when by the side of this image of jade, he saw a merchant presenting as his offering a fan of white silk;[5] and the tears of sorrow involuntarily filled his eyes and fell down.

A former king of the country had sent to Central India and got a slip of the patra tree,[6] which he planted by the side of the hall of Buddha, where a tree grew up to the height of about 200 cubits. As it bent on one side towards the south-east, the king, fearing it would fall, propped it with a post eight or nine spans round. The tree began to grow at the very heart of the prop, where it met (the trunk); (a shoot) pierced through the post, and went down to the ground, where it entered and formed roots, that rose (to the surface) and were about four spans round. Although the post was split in the middle, the outer portions kept hold (of the shoot), and people did not remove them. Beneath the tree there has been built a vihara, in which there is an image (of Buddha) seated, which the monks and commonalty reverence and look up to without ever becoming wearied. In the city there has been reared also the vihara of Buddha's tooth, on which, as well as on the other, the seven precious substances have been employed.

The king practises the Brahmanical purifications, and the sincerity of the faith and reverence of the population inside the city are also great. Since the establishment of government in the kingdom there has been no famine or scarcity, no revolution or disorder. In the treasuries of the monkish communities there are many precious stones, and the priceless manis. One of the kings (once) entered one of those treasuries, and when he looked all round and saw the priceless pearls, his covetous greed was excited, and he wished to take them to himself by force. In three days, however, he came to himself, and immediately went and bowed his head to the ground in the midst of the monks, to show his repentance of the evil thought. As a sequel to this, he informed the monks (of what had been in his mind), and desired them to make a regulation that from that day forth the king should not be allowed to enter the treasury and see (what it contained), and that no bhikshu should enter it till after he had been in orders for a period of full forty years.[7]

In the city there are many Vaisya elders and Sabaean[8] merchants, whose houses are stately and beautiful. The lanes and passages are kept in good order. At the heads of the four principal streets there have been built

124

preaching halls, where, on the eighth, fourteenth, and fifteenth days of the month, they spread carpets, and set forth a pulpit, while the monks and commonalty from all quarters come together to hear the Law. The people say that in the kingdom there may be altogether sixty thousand monks, who get their food from their common stores. The king, besides, prepares elsewhere in the city a common supply of food for five or six thousand more. When any want, they take their great bowls, and go (to the place of distribution), and take as much as the vessels will hold, all returning with them full.

The tooth of Buddha is always brought forth in the middle of the third month. Ten days beforehand the king grandly caparisons a large elephant, on which he mounts a man who can speak distinctly, and is dressed in royal robes, to beat a large drum, and make the following proclamation:--"The Bodhisattva, during three Asankhyeya-kalpas,[9] manifested his activity, and did not spare his own life. He gave up kingdom, city, wife, and son; he plucked out his eyes and gave them to another;[10] he cut off a piece of his own flesh to ransom the life of a dove;[10] he cut off his head and gave it as an alms;[11] he gave his body to feed a starving tigress;[11] he grudged not his marrow and his brains. In many such ways as these did he undergo pain for the sake of all living. And so it was, that, having become Buddha, he continued in the world for forty-five years, preaching his Law, teaching and transforming, so that those who had no rest found rest, and the unconverted were converted. When his connexion with the living was completed,[12] he attained to pari-nirvana (and died). Since that event, for 1497 years, the light of the world has gone out,[13] and all living beings have had long-continued sadness. Behold! ten days after this, Buddha's tooth will be brought forth, and taken to the Abhayagiri-vihara. Let all and each, whether monks or laics, who wish to amass merit for themselves, make the roads smooth and in good condition, grandly adorn the lanes and by-ways, and provide abundant store of flowers and incense to be used as offerings to it."

When this proclamation is over, the king exhibits, so as to line both sides of the road, the five hundred different bodily forms in which the Bodhisattva has in the course of his history appeared:--here as Sudana,[14] there as Sama;[15] now as the king of elephants;[16] and then as a stag or a horse.[16] All these figures are brightly coloured and grandly executed, looking as if

125

they were alive. After this the tooth of Buddha is brought forth, and is carried along in the middle of the road. Everywhere on the way offerings are presented to it, and thus it arrives at the hall of Buddha in the Abhayagiri-vihara. There monks and laics are collected in crowds. They burn incense, light lamps, and perform all the prescribed services, day and night without ceasing, till ninety days have been completed, when (the tooth) is returned to the vihara within the city. On fast-days the door of that vihara is opened, and the forms of ceremonial reverence are observed according to the rules.

Forty le to the east of the Abhayagiri-vihara there is a hill, with a vihara on it, called the Chaitya,[17] where there may be 2000 monks. Among them there is a Sramana of great virtue, named Dharma-gupta,[18] honoured and looked up to by all the kingdom. He has lived for more than forty years in an apartment of stone, constantly showing such gentleness of heart, that he has brought snakes and rats to stop together in the same room, without doing one another any harm.

NOTES

[1] It is desirable to translate {.} {.}, for which "inhabitants" or "people" is elsewhere sufficient, here by "human inhabitants." According to other accounts Singhala was originally occupied by Rakshasas or Rakshas, "demons who devour men," and "beings to be feared," monstrous cannibals or anthropophagi, the terror of the shipwrecked mariner. Our author's "spirits" {.} {.} were of a gentler type. His dragons or nagas have come before us again and again.

[2] That Sakyamuni ever visited Ceylon is to me more than doubtful. Hardy, in M. B., pp. 207-213, has brought together the legends of three visits,--in the first, fifth, and eighth years of his Buddhaship. It is plain, however, from Fa-hien's narrative, that in the beginning of our fifth century, Buddhism prevailed throughout the island. Davids in the last chapter of his "Buddhism" ascribes its introduction to one of Asoka's missions, after the Council of Patna, under his son Mahinda, when Tissa, "the delight of the gods," was king (B.C. 250-230).

[3] This would be what is known as "Adam's peak," having, according to Hardy (pp. 211, 212, notes), the three names of Selesumano, Samastakuta, and Samanila. "There is an indentation on the top of it," a superficial hollow, 5 feet 3 3/4 inches long, and about 2 1/2 feet wide. The Hindus regard it as the footprint of Siva; the Mohameddans, as that of Adam; and the Buddhists, as in the text,--as having been made by Buddha.

[4] Meaning "The Fearless Hill." There is still the Abhayagiri tope, the highest in Ceylon, according to Davids, 250 feet in height, and built about B.C. 90, by Watta Gamini, in whose reign, about 160 years after the Council of Patna, and 330 years after the death of Sakyamuni, the Tripitaka was first reduced to writing in Ceylon;-- "Buddhism," p. 234.

[5] We naturally suppose that the merchant-offerer was a Chinese, as indeed the Chinese texts say, and the fan such as Fa-hien had seen and used in his native land.

[6] This should be the pippala, or bodhidruma, generally spoken of, in connexion with Buddha, as the Bo tree, under which he attained to the Buddhaship. It is strange our author should have confounded them as he seems to do. In what we are told of the tree here, we have, no doubt, his account of the planting, growth, and preservation of the famous Bo tree, which still exists in Ceylon. It has been stated in a previous note that Asoka's son, Mahinda, went as the apostle of Buddhism to Ceylon. By-and-by he sent for his sister Sanghamitta, who had entered the order at the same time as himself, and whose help was needed, some of the king's female relations having signified their wish to become nuns. On leaving India, she took with her a branch of the sacred Bo tree at Buddha Gaya, under which Sakyamuni had become Buddha. Of how the tree has grown and still lives we have an account in Davids' "Buddhism." He quotes the words of Sir Emerson Tennent, that it is "the oldest historical tree in the world;" but this must be denied if it be true, as Eitel says, that the tree at Buddha Gaya, from which the slip that grew to be this tree was taken more than 2000 years ago, is itself still living in its place. We must conclude that Fa-hien, when in Ceylon, heard neither of Mahinda nor Sanghamitta.

[7] Compare what is said in chap. xvi, about the inquiries made at monasteries as to the standing of visitors in the monkhood, and duration of their ministry.

[8] The phonetic values of the two Chinese characters here are in Sanskrit sa; and va, bo or bha. "Sabaean" is Mr. Beal's reading of them, probably correct. I suppose the merchants were Arabs, forerunners of the so-called Moormen, who still form so important a part of the mercantile community in Ceylon.

[9] A Kalpa, we have seen, denotes a great period of time; a period during which a physical universe is formed and destroyed. Asankhyeya denotes the highest sum for which a conventional term exists;-- according to Chinese calculations equal to one followed by seventeen ciphers; according to Thibetan and Singhalese, equal to one followed by ninety-seven ciphers. Every Maha-kalpa consists of four Asankhyeya- kalpas. Eitel, p. 15.

[10] See chapter ix.

[11] See chapter xi.

[12] He had been born in the Sakya house, to do for the world what the character of all his past births required, and he had done it.

[13] They could no more see him, the World-honoured one. Compare the Sacred Books of the East, vol. xi, Buddhist Suttas, pp. 89, 121, and note on p. 89.

[14] Sudana or Sudatta was the name of the Bodhisattva in the birth which preceded his appearance as Sakyamuni or Gotama, when he became the Supreme Buddha. This period is known as the Vessantara Jataka, of which Hardy, M. B., pp. 116-124, gives a long account; see also "Buddhist Birth Stories," the Nidana Katha, p. 158. In it, as Sudana, he fulfilled "the Perfections," his distinguishing attribute being entire self-renunciation and alms-giving, so that in the Nidana Katha is made to say ("Buddhist Birth

Stories," p. 159):--

"This earth, unconscious though she be, and ignorant of joy or grief, Even she by my free-giving's mighty power was shaken seven times."

Then, when he passed away, he appeared in the Tushita heaven, to enter in due time the womb of Maha-maya, and be born as Sakyamuni.

[15] I take the name Sama from Beal's revised version. He says in a note that the Sama Jataka, as well as the Vessantara, is represented in the Sanchi sculptures. But what the Sama Jataka was I do not yet know. But adopting this name, the two Chinese characters in the text should be translated "the change into Sama." Remusat gives for them, "la transformation en eclair;" Beal, in his first version, "his appearance as a bright flash of light;" Giles, "as a flash of lightning." Julien's Methode does not give the phonetic value in Sanskrit of {.}.

[16] In an analysis of the number of times and the different forms in which Sakyamuni had appeared in his Jataka births, given by Hardy (M. B., p. 100), it is said that he had appeared six times as an elephant; ten times as a deer; and four times as a horse.

[17] Chaitya is a general term designating all places and objects of religious worship which have a reference to ancient Buddhas, and including therefore Stupas and temples as well as sacred relics, pictures, statues, &c. It is defined as "a fane," "a place for worship and presenting offerings." Eitel, p. 141. The hill referred to is the sacred hill of Mihintale, about eight miles due east of the Bo tree;-- Davids' Buddhism, pp. 230, 231.

[18] Eitel says (p. 31): "A famous ascetic, the founder of a school, which flourished in Ceylon, A.D. 400." But Fa-hien gives no intimation of Dharma-gupta's founding a school.

CHAPTER XXXIX

CREMATION OF AN ARHAT. SERMON OF A DEVOTEE.

South of the city seven le there is a vihara, called the Maha-vihara, where 3000 monks reside. There had been among them a Sramana, of such lofty virtue, and so holy and pure in his observance of the disciplinary rules, that the people all surmised that he was an Arhat. When he drew near his end, the king came to examine into the point; and having assembled the monks according to rule, asked whether the bhikshu had attained to the full degree of Wisdom.[1] They answered in the affirmative, saying that he was an Arhat. The king accordingly, when he died, buried him after the fashion of an Arhat, as the regular rules prescribed. Four of five le east from the vihara there was reared a great pile of firewood, which might be more than thirty cubits square, and the same in height. Near the top were laid sandal, aloe, and other kinds of fragrant wood.

On the four sides (of the pile) they made steps by which to ascend it. With clean white hair-cloth, almost like silk, they wrapped (the body) round and round.[2] They made a large carriage-frame, in form like our funeral car, but without the dragons and fishes.[3]

At the time of the cremation, the king and the people, in multitudes from all quarters, collected together, and presented offerings of flowers and incense. While they were following the car to the burial- ground,[4] the king himself presented flowers and incense. When this was finished, the car was lifted on the pile, all over which oil of sweet basil was poured, and then a light was applied. While the fire was blazing, every one, with a reverent heart, pulled off his upper garment, and threw it, with his feather-fan and umbrella, from a distance into the midst of the flames, to assist the burning. When the cremation was over, they collected and preserved the bones, and proceeded to erect a tope. Fa-hien had not arrived in time (to see the distinguished Shaman) alive, and only saw his burial.

At that time the king,[5] who was a sincere believer in the Law of Buddha and wished to build a new vihara for the monks, first convoked a great assembly. After giving the monks a meal of rice, and presenting his offerings (on the occasion), he selected a pair of first-rate oxen, the horns of which were grandly decorated with gold, silver, and the precious substances. A golden plough had been provided, and the king himself turned up a furrow on the four sides of the ground within which the building was supposed to be. He then endowed the community of the monks with the population, fields, and houses, writing the grant on plates of metal, (to the effect) that from that time onwards, from generation to generation, no one should venture to annul or alter it.

In this country Fa-hien heard an Indian devotee, who was reciting a Sutra from the pulpit, say:--"Buddha's alms-bowl was at first in Vaisali, and now it is in Gandhara.[6] After so many hundred years' (he gave, when Fa-hien heard him, the exact number of years, but he has forgotten it), "it will go to Western Tukhara;[7] after so many hundred years, to Khoten; after so many hundred years, to Kharachar;[8] after so many hundred years, to the land of Han; after so many hundred years, it will come to Sinhala; and after so many hundred years, it will return to Central India. After that, it will ascend to the Tushita heaven; and when the Bodhisattva Maitreya sees it, he will say with a sigh, 'The alms-bowl of Sakyamuni Buddha is come;' and with all the devas he will present to it flowers and incense for seven days. When these have expired, it will return to Jambudvipa, where it will be received by the king of the sea nagas, and taken into his naga palace. When Maitreya shall be about to attain to perfect Wisdom (and become Buddha), it will again separate into four bowls,[9] which will return to the top of mount Anna,[9] whence they came. After Maitreya has become Buddha, the four deva kings will again think of the Buddha (with their bowls as they did in the case of the previous Buddha). The thousand Buddhas of this Bhadra-kalpa, indeed, will all use the same alms-bowl; and when the bowl has disappeared, the Law of Buddha will go on gradually to be extinguished. After that extinction has taken place, the life of man will be shortened, till it is only a period of five years. During this period of a five years' life, rice, butter, and oil will all vanish away, and men will become exceedingly wicked. The grass and trees which they lay hold of will change into swords and clubs, with which they will hurt, cut, and kill one another. Those among them on whom there is blessing will withdraw from society among the hills; and when the wicked have exterminated one another, they will again come forth, and say among themselves, 'The men of former times enjoyed a very great longevity; but through becoming exceedingly wicked, and doing all lawless things, the length of our life has been shortened and reduced even to five years. Let us now unite together in the practice of what is good, cherishing a gentle and sympathising heart, and carefully cultivating good faith and righteousness. When each one in this way practises that faith and righteousness, life will go on to double its length till it reaches 80,000 years. When Maitreya appears in the world, and begins to turn the wheel of his Law, he will in the first place save those among the disciples of the Law left by the Sakya who have quitted their families, and those who have accepted the three Refuges, undertaken the five Prohibitions and the eight Abstinences, and given offerings to the three Precious Ones; secondly and thirdly, he will save those between whom and conversion there is a connexion transmitted from the past.'"[10]

(Such was the discourse), and Fa-hien wished to write it down as a portion of doctrine; but the man said, "This is taken from no Sutra, it is only the utterance of my own mind."

NOTES

[1] Possibly, "and asked the bhikshu," &c. I prefer the other way of construing, however.

[2] It seems strange that this should have been understood as a wrapping of the immense pyre with the cloth. There is nothing in the text to necessitate such a version, but the contrary. Compare "Buddhist Suttas," pp. 92, 93.

[3] See the description of a funeral car and its decorations in the Sacred Books of the East, vol. xxviii, the Li Ki, Book XIX. Fa-hien's {.} {.}, "in this (country)," which I have expressed by "our," shows that whatever notes of this cremation he had taken at the time, the account in the text was composed after his return to China, and when he had the usages there in his mind and perhaps before his eyes. This disposes of all difficulty occasioned by the "dragons" and "fishes." The {.} at the end is merely the concluding particle.

[4] The pyre served the purpose of a burial-ground or grave, and hence our

author writes of it as such.

[5] This king must have been Maha-nana (A.D. 410-432). In the time of his predecessor, Upatissa (A.D. 368-410), the pitakas were first translated into Singhalese. Under Maha-nana, Buddhaghosha wrote his commentaries. Both were great builders of viharas. See the Mahavansa, pp. 247, foll.

[6] See chapter xii. Fa-hien had seen it at Purushapura, which Eitel says was "the ancient capital of Gandhara."

[7] Western Tukhara ({.} {.}) is the same probably as the Tukhara ({.}) of chapter xii, a king of which is there described as trying to carry off the bowl from Purushapura.

[8] North of the Bosteng lake at the foot of the Thien-shan range (E. H., p. 56).

[9] See chap. xii, note 9. Instead of "Anna" the Chinese recensions have Vina; but Vina or Vinataka, and Ana for Sudarsana are names of one or other of the concentric circles of rocks surrounding mount Meru, the fabled home of the deva guardians of the bowl.

[10] That is, those whose Karma in the past should be rewarded by such conversion in the present.

CHAPTER XL

AFTER TWO YEARS TAKES SHIP FOR CHINA. DISASTROUS PASSAGE TO JAVA; AND THENCE TO CHINA; ARRIVES AT SHAN-TUNG; AND GOES TO NANKING. CONCLUSION OR L'ENVOI BY ANOTHER WRITER.

Fa-hien abode in this country two years; and, in addition (to his acquisitions in Patna), succeeded in getting a copy of the Vinaya- pitaka of the Mahisasakah (school);[1] the Dirghagama and Samyuktagama[2] (Sutras); and also the Samyukta-sanchaya-pitaka;[3]-- all being works

133

unknown in the land of Han. Having obtained these Sanskrit works, he took passage in a large merchantman, on board of which there were more than 200 men, and to which was attached by a rope a smaller vessel, as a provision against damage or injury to the large one from the perils of the navigation. With a favourable wind, they proceeded eastwards for three days, and then they encountered a great wind. The vessel sprang a leak and the water came in. The merchants wished to go to the small vessel; but the men on board it, fearing that too many would come, cut the connecting rope. The merchants were greatly alarmed, feeling their risk of instant death. Afraid that the vessel would fill, they took their bulky goods and threw them into the water. Fa-hien also took his pitcher[4] and washing-basin, with some other articles, and cast them into the sea; but fearing that the merchants would cast overboard his books and images, he could only think with all his heart of Kwan-she-yin,[5] and commit his life to (the protection of) the church of the land of Han,[6] (saying in effect), "I have travelled far in search of our Law. Let me, by your dread and supernatural (power), return from my wanderings, and reach my resting-place!"

In this way the tempest[7] continued day and night, till on the thirteenth day the ship was carried to the side of an island, where, on the ebbing of the tide, the place of the leak was discovered, and it was stopped, on which the voyage was resumed. On the sea (hereabouts) there are many pirates, to meet with whom is speedy death. The great ocean spreads out, a boundless expanse. There is no knowing east or west; only by observing the sun, moon, and stars was it possible to go forward. If the weather were dark and rainy, (the ship) went as she was carried by the wind, without any definite course. In the darkness of the night, only the great waves were to be seen, breaking on one another, and emitting a brightness like that of fire, with huge turtles and other monsters of the deep (all about). The merchants were full of terror, not knowing where they were going. The sea was deep and bottomless, and there was no place where they could drop anchor and stop. But when the sky became clear, they could tell east and west, and (the ship) again went forward in the right direction. If she had come on any hidden rock, there would have been no way of escape.

After proceeding in this way for rather more than ninety days, they arrived at a country called Java-dvipa, where various forms of error and Brahmanism are flourishing, while Buddhism in it is not worth speaking of. After staying there for five months, (Fa-hien) again embarked in another large merchantman, which also had on board more than 200 men. They carried provisions for fifty days, and commenced the voyage on the sixteenth day of the fourth month.

Fa-hien kept his retreat on board the ship. They took a course to the north-east, intending to fetch Kwang-chow. After more than a month, when the night-drum had sounded the second watch, they encountered a black wind and tempestuous rain, which threw the merchants and passengers into consternation. Fa-hien again with all his heart directed his thoughts to Kwan-she-yin and the monkish communities of the land of Han; and, through their dread and mysterious protection, was preserved to day-break. After day-break, the Brahmans deliberated together and said, "It is having this Sramana on board which has occasioned our misfortune and brought us this great and bitter suffering. Let us land the bhikshu and place him on some island-shore. We must not for the sake of one man allow ourselves to be exposed to such imminent peril." A patron of Fa-hien, however, said to them, "If you land the bhikshu, you must at the same time land me; and if you do not, then you must kill me. If you land this Sramana, when I get to the land of Han, I will go to the king, and inform against you. The king also reveres and believes the Law of Buddha, and honours the bhikshus." The merchants hereupon were perplexed, and did not dare immediately to land (Fa-hien).

At this time the sky continued very dark and gloomy, and the sailing-masters looked at one another and made mistakes. More than seventy days passed (from their leaving Java), and the provisions and water were nearly exhausted. They used the salt-water of the sea for cooking, and carefully divided the (fresh) water, each man getting two pints. Soon the whole was nearly gone, and the merchants took counsel and said, "At the ordinary rate of sailing we ought to have reached Kwang-chow, and now the time is passed by many days;--must we not have held a wrong course?" Immediately they directed the ship to the north- west, looking out for land; and after sailing day and night for twelve days, they reached the shore on the south of mount Lao,[8] on the borders of the prefecture of Ch'ang-kwang,[8] and immediately got good water and vegetables. They had passed through many perils and hardships, and had been in a state of anxious apprehension for many days together; and now suddenly arriving at this shore, and seeing those (well-known) vegetables, the lei and kwoh,[9] they knew indeed that it was the land of Han. Not seeing, however, any inhabitants nor any traces of them, they did not know whereabouts they were. Some said that they had not yet got to Kwang-chow, and others that they had passed it. Unable to come to a definite conclusion, (some of them) got into a small boat and entered a creek, to look for some one of whom they might ask what the place was. They found two hunters, whom they brought back with them, and then called on Fa-hien to act as interpreter and question them. Fa-hien first spoke assuringly to them, and then slowly and distinctly asked them, "Who are you?" They replied, "We are disciples of Buddha?" He then asked, "What are you looking for among these hills?" They began to lie,[10] and said, "To-morrow is the fifteenth day of the seventh month. We wanted to get some peaches to present[11] to Buddha." He asked further, "What country is this?" They replied, "This is the border of the prefecture of Ch'ang-kwang, a part of Ts'ing-chow under the (ruling) House of Tsin." When they heard this, the merchants were glad, immediately asked for (a portion of) their money and goods, and sent men to Ch'ang-kwang city.

The prefect Le E was a reverent believer in the Law of Buddha. When he heard that a Sramana had arrived in a ship across the sea, bringing with him books and images, he immediately came to the seashore with an escort to meet (the traveller), and receive the books and images, and took them back with him to the seat of his government. On this the merchants went back in the direction of Yang-chow;[12] (but) when (Fa-hien) arrived at Ts'ing-chow, (the prefect there)[13] begged him (to remain with him) for a winter and a summer. After the summer retreat was ended, Fa-hien, having been separated for a long time from his (fellow-)masters, wished to hurry to Ch'ang-gan; but as the business which he had in hand was important, he went south to the Capital;[14] and at an interview with the masters (there) exhibited the Sutras and the collection of the Vinaya (which he had procured).

After Fa-hien set out from Ch'ang-gan, it took him six years to reach

Central India;[15] stoppages there extended over (other) six years; and on his return it took him three years to reach Ts'ing-chow. The countries through which he passed were a few under thirty. From the sandy desert westwards on to India, the beauty of the dignified demeanour of the monkhood and of the transforming influence of the Law was beyond the power of language fully to describe; and reflecting how our masters had not heard any complete account of them, he therefore (went on) without regarding his own poor life, or (the dangers to be encountered) on the sea upon his return, thus incurring hardships and difficulties in a double form. He was fortunate enough, through the dread power of the three Honoured Ones,[15] to receive help and protection in his perils; and therefore he wrote out an account of his experiences, that worthy readers might share with him in what he had heard and said.[15]

It was in the year Keah-yin,[16] the twelfth year of the period E-he of the (Eastern) Tsin dynasty, the year-star being in Virgo-Libra, in the summer, at the close of the period of retreat, that I met the devotee Fa-hien. On his arrival I lodged him with myself in the winter study,[17] and there, in our meetings for conversation, I asked him again and again about his travels. The man was modest and complaisant, and answered readily according to the truth. I thereupon advised him to enter into details where he had at first only given a summary, and he proceeded to relate all things in order from the beginning to the end. He said himself, "When I look back on what I have gone through, my heart is involuntarily moved, and the perspiration flows forth. That I encountered danger and trod the most perilous places, without thinking of or sparing myself, was because I had a definite aim, and thought of nothing but to do my best in my simplicity and straightforwardness. Thus it was that I exposed my life where death seemed inevitable, if I might accomplish but a ten-thousandth part of what I hoped." These words affected me in turn, and I thought:--"This man is one of those who have seldom been seen from ancient times to the present. Since the Great Doctrine flowed on to the East there has been no one to be compared with Hien in his forgetfulness of self and search for the Law. Henceforth I know that the influence of sincerity finds no obstacle, however great, which it does not overcome, and that force of will does not fail to accomplish whatever service it undertakes. Does not the accomplishing of such service arise from

137

forgetting (and disregarding) what is (generally) considered as important, and attaching importance to what is (generally) forgotten?

NOTES

[1] No. 1122 in Nanjio's Catalogue, translated into Chinese by Buddhajiva and a Chinese Sramana about A.D. 425. Mahisasakah means "the school of the transformed earth," or "the sphere within which the Law of Buddha is influential." The school is one of the subdivisions of the Sarvastivadah.

[2] Nanjio's 545 and 504. The Agamas are Sutras of the hinayana, divided, according to Eitel, pp. 4, 5, into four classes, the first or Dirghagamas (long Agamas) being treatises on right conduct, while the third class contains the Samyuktagamas (mixed Agamas).

[3] Meaning "Miscellaneous Collections;" a sort of fourth Pitaka. See Nanjio's fourth division of the Canon, containing Indian and Chinese miscellaneous works. But Dr. Davids says that no work of this name is known either in Sanskrit or Pali literature.

[4] We have in the text a phonetisation of the Sanskrit Kundika, which is explained in Eitel by the two characters that follow, as="washing basin," but two things evidently are intended.

[5] See chap. xvi, note 23.

[6] At his novitiate Fa-hien had sought the refuge of the "three Precious Ones" (the three Refuges {.} {.} of last chapter), of which the congregation or body of the monks was one; and here his thoughts turn naturally to the branch of it in China. His words in his heart were not exactly words of prayer, but very nearly so.

[7] In the text {.} {.}, ta-fung, "the great wind,"=the typhoon.

[8] They had got to the south of the Shan-tung promontory, and the foot of mount Lao, which still rises under the same name on the extreme south of

138

the peninsula, east from Keao Chow, and having the district of Tsieh-mih on the east of it. All the country there is included in the present Phing-too Chow of the department Lae-chow. The name Phing-too dates from the Han dynasty, but under the dynasty of the After Ch'e {.} {.}, (A.D. 479-501), it was changed into Ch'ang- kwang. Fa-hien may have lived, and composed the narrative of his travels, after the change of name was adopted. See the Topographical Tables of the different Dynasties ({.} {.} {.} {.} {.}), published in 1815.

[9] What these vegetables exactly were it is difficult to say; and there are different readings of the characters for them. Williams' Dictionary, under kwoh, brings the two names together in a phrase, but the rendering of it is simply "a soup of simples." For two or three columns here, however, the text appears to me confused and imperfect.

[10] I suppose these men were really hunters; and, when brought before Fa-hien, because he was a Sramana, they thought they would please him by saying they were disciples of Buddha. But what had disciples of Buddha to do with hunting and taking life? They were caught in their own trap, and said they were looking for peaches.

[11] The Chinese character here has occurred twice before, but in a different meaning and connexion. Remusat, Beal, and Giles take it as equivalent to "to sacrifice." But his followers do not "sacrifice" to Buddha. That is a priestly term, and should not be employed of anything done at Buddhistic services.

[12] Probably the present department of Yang-chow in Keang-soo; but as I have said in a previous note, the narrative does not go on so clearly as it generally does.

[13] Was, or could, this prefect be Le E?

[14] Probably not Ch'ang-gan, but Nan-king, which was the capital of the Eastern Tsin dynasty under another name.

[15] The whole of this paragraph is probably Fa-hien's own conclusion of his narrative. The second half of the second sentence, both in sentiment and style in the Chinese text, seems to necessitate our ascribing it to him, writing on the impulse of his own thoughts, in the same indirect form which he adopted for his whole narrative. There are, however, two peculiar phraseologies in it which might suggest the work of another hand. For the name India, where the first [15] is placed, a character is employed which is similarly applied nowhere else; and again, "the three Honoured Ones," at which the second [15] is placed, must be the same as "the three Precious Ones," which we have met with so often; unless we suppose that {.} {.} is printed in all the revisions for {.} {.}, "the World-honoured one," which has often occurred. On the whole, while I accept this paragraph as Fa-hien's own, I do it with some hesitation. That the following and concluding paragraph is from another hand, there can be no doubt. And it is as different as possible in style from the simple and straightforward narrative of Fa-hien.

[16] There is an error of date here, for which it is difficult to account. The year Keah-yin was A.D. 414; but that was the tenth year of the period E-he, and not the twelfth, the cyclical designation of which was Ping-shin. According to the preceding paragraph, Fa-hien's travels had occupied him fifteen years, so that counting from A.D. 399, the year Ke-hae, as that in which he set out, the year of his getting to Ts'ing-chow would have been Kwei-chow, the ninth year of the period E-he; and we might join on "This year Keah-yin" to that paragraph, as the date at which the narrative was written out for the bamboo-tablets and the silk, and then begins the Envoy, "In the twelfth year of E-he." This would remove the error as it stands at present, but unfortunately there is a particle at the end of the second date ({.}), which seems to tie the twelfth year of E-he to Keah-yin, as another designation of it. The "year-star" is the planet Jupiter, the revolution of which, in twelve years, constitutes "a great year." Whether it would be possible to fix exactly by mathematical calculation in what year Jupiter was in the Chinese zodiacal sign embracing part of both Virgo and Scorpio, and thereby help to solve the difficulty of the passage, I do not know, and in the meantime must leave that difficulty as I have found it.

[17] We do not know who the writer of the Envoy was. "The winter study

or library" would be the name of the apartment in his monastery or house, where he sat and talked with Fa-hien.

###

www.ingramcontent.com/pod-product-compliance
Lightning Source LLC
Chambersburg PA
CBHW060807100426
42813CB00004B/982

9 781989 743041